WOMEN AND DEPRESSION
A practical self-help guide

Deidre Sanders

SHELDON PRESS
LONDON

First published in Great Britain in 1984 by
Sheldon Press, SPCK, Marylebone Road, London NW1 4DU

Copyright © Deidre Sanders 1984

British Library Cataloguing in Publication Data

Sanders, Deidre
    Women and depression.—(Healthcare for women)
    1. Depression, Mental—Treatment 2. Women
    —Mental Health 3. Self-care, Health
    I. Title   II. Series
    616.85'2706   RC537

    ISBN 0–85969–418–6
    ISBN 0–85969–419–4 Pbk

Typeset by Bocardo Press Ltd, Cowley, Oxford

Printed in Great Britain by
Richard Clay (The Chaucer Press) Ltd
Bungay, Suffolk

I am very grateful to all the women who talked to me about their experiences of depression, even when doing so stirred up painful memories. Where I have quoted them, I have changed their names to protect their privacy.

Thank you, Pat and Patt, for your patience with the manuscript; Anne Dickson, for increasing my understanding; and Rick, for your help and sense of humour.

Contents

Introduction

Every year, one in five women takes tranquillizers at some time, usually for depression. Many more feel anxious and depressed but don't seek medical treatment – they just take another headache pill. Imagine the outcry there would be if we were talking about a virus that so affected millions upon millions of people every year.

Yet here we are, with what amounts to a plague in the land, and each individual sufferer tends to blame herself and feel guilty because she suffers from this common complaint. Nearly every woman I talked to for this book had been told by family and friends to snap out of it – as if her depression were something easily under her personal control. It's about as helpful as telling someone to snap out of influenza or a broken leg.

Women are at least twice as likely to suffer depression as men and, when so many succumb, there clearly must be some common factors at work. So any woman suffering from depression has absolutely no need to blame herself or feel that she is weak, incompetent or lacking in moral fibre.

However, no woman has to feel that it is all helplessly out of her control, either. While it is not possible just to snap out of depression, you can climb out steadily, in easy stages, and that's what this book is all about.

The word depression covers a huge range of feelings and illness. We may say we are depressed when we just have a down day. But some doctors maintain that true depression is only experienced by people who suffer from bio-chemical changes in the brain – known as endogenous depression. They maintain that everyone else who claims to be depressed is just unhappy. However, I reckon that if *you* feel you are depressed, if life seems to have lost all its zest or you feel you need tranquillizers, then you are down enough to need help.

While the GP doesn't hold the real answer to most women's anxiety and depression hidden in his prescription pad, a

1

minority who are suffering from very severe depression can be dramatically helped by treatment with anti-depressants. If in any doubt at all, seek your doctor's advice.

On the other hand, it would be unrealistic to expect to be happy all the time and run to the doctor every time we felt sad. Unhappiness is not an illness; it is a natural part of human experience. If we couldn't experience grief, we couldn't feel joy either – which can be exactly the effect of numbing ourselves with drugs.

If we are miserable because of very real problems in our lives, we are not ill. We need help to change what can be changed, courage to accept what can't, insight to tell the difference – and none of that comes out of a bottle.

I believe that with enlightened self-help and support, most women now taking tranquillizers could stop doing so and never look back. However, this usually means that those around her must be prepared to make a few changes in the way they behave, too. I do realise that there are many families struggling desperately to help a depressed member, and suffering themselves in the process. However, while writing this book I talked to many women who had suffered depression. A striking similarity in the accounts they gave was the ostrich-like attitude of some husbands and families, who too often tried to keep their heads firmly in the sand and ignore the woman's pain.

Yet the greatest protection a woman can have against depression is known to be a close and confiding relationship with her husband or boyfriend or, failing that, with another member of her family. Saying 'Snap out of it', or turning on the TV when she needs to talk, is like refusing penicillin to someone with pneumonia. Serious depression can be a fatal illness – one in five attempt suicide – and family and friends should be aware of this and watch out for danger signals.

Even quite mild depression can have a tenacious grip. We can't simply flick a mental switch and say 'Tomorrow I will wake up cheerful, life will have regained its colour.'

One reason for this is that we cannot divorce our mind and emotions from our body. How we feel causes physical changes in our body, and changes in our body can affect our emotions.

Introduction

When we talk of being tense we usually mean we feel irritable, on edge, unhappy, liable to get a headache. And when we feel like this our muscles are quite literally tense. If we can learn to relax them, we start to feel less irritable, more cheerful, and our headache will probably disappear.

We can all accept that most physical disease takes time to put right, and once we understand that there is a bodily element to anxiety and depression, it becomes obvious that we cannot expect these to disappear overnight, either.

The second main reason why depression can't be cleared in a trice is that it rarely has just one cause. Each of these contributing causes can be likened to a piece of a jigsaw puzzle. For some the puzzle is made up of two or three large pieces which may all fit together quite early in life. Other people cruise along for years seeming able to cope with many different pressures, then something quite small may prove to be the final piece of their jigsaw, completing the picture of depression for them.

Most of the chapters in this book are about common pieces in the jigsaw puzzle. The earlier ones are relevant to most women (and to many men suffering from depression). Others, such as the chapter on childbirth and depression, will apply only to a minority – though to a sizeable minority – of women. Most chapters end with a plan of practical action to help you tackle specific pieces of the jigsaw that go to make up your depression.

You won't clear your depression overnight. I wouldn't advise anyone to throw away their tranquillizers tomorrow, but today can be the beginning of the end of your depression.

D.S.   1984

ONE

Not All in the Mind

Many women feel guilty about being depressed. They worry that it shows they are weak, incompetent failures, and are alarmed to find their feelings so out of control. 'Why can't I get a grip on myself?' they ask.

If you feel like that, stop blaming yourself. Depression often strikes down precisely those who have always been very much in control of their lives – like Mary.

Mary, the usually cheery, bustling mother of three sons, is happily married to a successful builder. When tragedy struck and leukaemia was diagnosed in their six-year-old boy, everyone admired her strength. Not knowing if her son would live, she made endless trips to hospital, watched him suffer painful treatment, and still looked after her husband, her other children and her home.

A year after her son came out of hospital she startled family, friends and neighbours by sliding into a deep depression. She went to her doctor, said 'I don't feel very well', and burst into tears.

> For a couple of weeks I didn't get dressed. I wandered about in my housecoat unable to do anything. I heard voices. I would be more or less all right during the day but sitting down in the evening, the panicky feeling would build up and up as we sat there with the TV and fire on, and it was all dark outside. I felt closed in. I couldn't get out.
>
> I think guilt was one cause of it. I felt I was to blame for Kevin getting leukaemia. If only I'd gone to the doctor sooner, if only I'd done this or that ... always 'ifs'. It might have helped to talk to my husband about it, but he's not that sort. We'd always kept our feelings to ourselves. He showed the classic attitude – I was supposed to put up with it or snap out of it. 'You've got your children and your home,' he'd say. 'What more do you want?'

While we look down on depression as a weakness, stress

has almost become a fashionable ailment. Successful businessmen showing signs of stress are ordered to rest at expensive health farms. To suffer from stress shows how hard they've been working and how successful they are. But look at the following lists of symptoms of stress and tick any that trouble you.

Anyone suffering from five or more of them[1] needs to take action to reduce stress before it can cause depression.

Mental symptoms of stress

Constantly feeling irritable ☐

Often feeling helpless and unable to cope ☐

Lack of interest in life and other people ☐

Constant or recurrent fear of illness ☐

Poor memory and concentration ☐

Feeling a failure ☐

Feeling guilt or worthlessness, hating yourself ☐

Finding it difficult to make decisions ☐

Feeling that your appearance has altered and you are ugly ☐

Being conscious of bottling up rage or anger ☐

Finding it difficult to let go and laugh ☐

Feeling you are the target of other people's dislike or enmity ☐

Feeling neglected or let down by people you rely on ☐

Dreading the future, feeling hopeless ☐

Feeling you have failed as a partner or as a parent ☐

Feeling you have no-one whom you can really confide in ☐

Intense fear of open or enclosed spaces, of being alone or of death ☐

Physical symptoms of stress

Lack of appetite ☐

Craving for food when under pressure ☐

Frequent indigestion, such as heartburn ☐

Constipation or diarrhoea ☐

Insomnia ☐

Constant tiredness ☐

Sweating for no good reason ☐

Nervous tics, tendency to touch face and/or
hair repeatedly ☐

Nail-biting ☐

Cramps and muscular spasms ☐

Nausea ☐

Feelings of breathlessness when you haven't
exerted yourself ☐

Fainting spells ☐

Frequent crying or desire to cry ☐

Loss of sex drive, or other sexual problems ☐

Being unable to sit without fidgeting ☐

High blood pressure ☐

What is stress?

Stress is simply the reaction of body and mind to any change, good or bad.

We all need a certain amount of stress, or stimulus, in life. When we talk about people suffering from stress we mean from too much stress, or 'distress', in the same way that 'having a temperature' means having a high temperature.

Some people adapt well to change, positively thriving on challenge and coping easily with life's downs as well as ups. Most of us, however, are better at dealing with pleasant changes than with turns for the worse. We're more likely to suffer from distress at these times.

How we react depends on our individual body chemistry. But in all of us, when facing any very stressful situation the 'fight or flight' reaction appears. We literally prepare to fight or run away: muscles tense, adrenalin and noradrenalin are released into the blood, stored food is quickly converted into sugar and fat droplets to give energy. Breathing accelerates to provide the necessary extra oxygen. The heart pumps faster to fuel muscles with blood, and blood pressure rises.

The skin sweats to cool the body, and there's a tendency to turn pale as blood is diverted to muscles and tiny blood vessels near the skin surface contract. The pupils of the eyes expand enabling us to see better.

Tense muscles discharge lactic acid into the blood, triggering yet more anxiety. The more tense, excited, angry or frightened we are, the more 'wound-up' we become. Blood is diverted from other areas of the body. The digestive system slows down or stops. Saliva glands dry up. Blood vessels in the kidneys and abdomen contract.

We all recognize a pounding heart, panting breath, dry mouth, hollow stomach, and white, sweating skin from times of preparing for battle – before an exam, an interview, an anticipated row, or if we have to face a dangerous animal or enemy, or snatch a toddler from the path of a car.

After we have dealt with an emergency, the body quickly returns to the normal rest-and-digest condition that controls rest, sleep, digestion, stores up supplies in the body and keeps everything smoothly ticking over. It also makes up for the sudden demands of the fight or flight reaction. But this process takes time. The less fit we are, the longer it takes.

But modern stresses rarely consist of sudden life-or-death emergencies; things are less clear-cut. We may hate our job, but have to put up with it. We may be unemployed and unable to find work. We may live in a tower block with toddlers and have no hope of a house with a garden for years.

There is no moment of relief to trigger a return to rest-and-digest. We bottle up our anger, frustration and unhappiness, and stay wound-up.

With a body thus tuned to continual stress, high blood pressure stays; we may get heart and circulation problems.

The shut-down digestive system develops ulcers, colitis, diarrhoea and constipation. Tense muscles cause aches, pains and headaches. With the body's defence mechanism occupied elsewhere, infections and allergic symptoms are more likely. Bio-chemical changes in the brain sustain the feeling of anxiety.

This stage of stress is called 'the adaptation stage'. The body tries to adapt to the long-term stress, but cannot do so and remain healthy. The various symptoms produced create further stress: work suffers, tempers fray, sex-drive diminishes, pleasure disappears. We experience panic attacks – this is fight-or-flight working at full throttle – we feel a failure and have crying spells.

The adaptation stage can be brief or it can last for twenty years, depending on heredity, diet and exercise, our outlook on life, emotional support from friends and family, and the arrival of new pressures or crisis.

If nothing is done or nothing happens to relieve the stress, we may finally succumb to severe depression.

As yet research has produced no hard-and-fast conclusions about depression and bio-chemical changes in the brain, but it seems that chemicals called amines affect the pleasure and pain centres in the brain. When unrelieved stress unbalances amine levels, we become unable to experience pleasure – in other words, depressed.

Reactive depression

Doctors often divide depression into two types: reactive and endogenous. Reactive depression is about four times the more common of the two and is nearly always accompanied by anxiety. It affects more women than men, but this does not mean that men don't suffer from stress. They tend to show it in different ways – anxiety or 'nerves' in women may be a peptic ulcer for men, depression may be alcoholism – but men probably suffer as much as women.

Reactive depression is a reaction to some change involving a sense of loss. Sometimes this loss may not be obvious. But even the move to a bigger house in a more pleasant neighbourhood may mean losing old neighbours; a better-paid job may mean less freedom.

Reactive depression marred the early days of Penny and Graham's marriage. It was a second marriage for both and, when planning it, they were thrilled at the prospect of being together at last. But Penny found she was depressed from the day they got back from the honeymoon.

We came back and packed for the move in an incredible rush. After cooking meals and making beds for my brothers who were helping I was shattered. Then Graham went to work, my brothers went home, my son was at school and I was suddenly alone in this enormous house. I thought 'My God, what do I do now?'

Our relationship was super, and in many ways my life was much happier, but I'd left everything I had ever known. Family, friends, work, home-town. For six months I cried every day. I'd never done that before. I'd never nagged before but I became like a crotchety old woman, saying nasty things and then trying to brush them aside as if I hadn't.

I think the main problem was loneliness. Before marrying, I had worked full time and we went out two or three evenings a week. Here, I had no job, we were not going out, and I was stuck in looking at four walls. I'd been used to people popping in and out all day. Here, I turned on the TV just to have some sound around me.

Finally, it all boiled over and I told Graham that my life was empty. It was he who suggested going to see my doctor, who helped me enormously.

Two American doctors[2] have given ratings to the sort of changes that can cause reactive depression and these are listed below. If you score 160 or more you are likely to be showing signs of distress, though this can vary enormously. If you have been bottling up your feelings for some time, a relatively minor event could be the straw to break the camel's back. You might feel far more upset by a child leaving home, for example, if you were a lone parent and this your only child than if you were happily married and had two more children still at home.

Stress of adjusting to change within a six-month period

Death of husband or wife	100
Divorce	73
Marital separation	65
Jail sentence	63
Death of close member of family	63
Illness or injury	53
Marriage	50
Loss of job	47
Reconciliation with marriage partner	45
Retirement	45
Health problem of close member of family	44
Pregnancy	40
Sex problems	39
Addition to family	39
Major change at work	39
Change of financial status	38
Death of a close friend	37
Change in type of work	36
Increase in number of marital arguments	35
Large mortgage take out	31
Mortgage or loan foreclosed	30
Changes of responsibilities at work	29
Child leaves home	29
In-law problems	29
Major personal achievement realised	28
Spouse stops or starts work	26
Starting or leaving school	26
Change in living conditions	25
Change in personal habits	24
Trouble with employer	23
Change in work hours	20

Endogenous depression

Endogenous depression seems to arrive out of the blue; the result of years of unresolved stress, with the causes long buried. Bio-chemical changes underlie this form of depression which can also be caused by a disturbed hormone balance, possibly during childbirth or the menopause, after taking certain drugs, with glandular disorders, after severe injuries and operations, and with some diseases.

The symptoms are usually more physical, and more severe, than in reactive depression. The onset tends to occur later in life, often to people who have always seemed very well-controlled. It affects only one in five depressed people, but is as common among men as women.

Victims of endogenous depression tend to think and move very slowly, feeling worse in the morning and better as the day goes on. Reactive depression is usually worse in the evening.

Endogenous depressives go off food, while reactive depressives often eat more, for comfort. Endogenous depressives may wake early in the morning, while reactives have difficulty in going to sleep but wake at the normal time.

ACTION PLAN

Relaxation techniques effectively interrupt the stress

cycle. So learning to relax can cause a dramatic improvement in your mental and emotional well-being particularly if you are suffering from reactive depression.

Tense muscles give off lactic acid which triggers more feelings of anxiety, and we may be unconsciously holding some sets of muscles tense all day long. If you learn to relax, your body can resume its healthy rest and digest mode instead of remaining trapped in the fight or flight reaction. Tranquillizers often act by relaxing muscles; we can learn to do this ourselves, without drugs.

I am not saying that if you are seriously depressed you should do these exercises *instead* of seeing your doctor but, if you show interest, most doctors will happily guide you in learning natural methods of stress control. These methods may be instead of tranquillizers, as Penny's doctors recommended, or in addition to a course of anti-depressants, according to your needs.

Breathe deeply
When we are aroused our breath comes in short, sharp pants. Instead of filling our lungs fully, we use our upper chest only. The habit of always breathing shallowly can trigger off or increase sensations of anxiety.

There is also a tendency when panting to make in-breaths longer and deeper than out-breaths. Try imitating the breathing of someone panting with fear and you will notice this. This breathing pattern is now suspected to lie behind some stress-related illness. When practising deep-breathing techniques, concentrate on the out-breaths; make them longer than the in-breaths.

First thing in the morning, last thing at night, before or after meals, and any time you feel yourself growing tense, your breathing speeding up, your heart pounding, try deep breathing.

Straighten your head and shoulders, lift your rib cage up out of your waist so that your diaphragm can expand fully, and breathe deeply. Breathe in through your nose and out through your mouth. I breathe in to a slow count of six and out to a slow count of eight, but find the rate that suits you – so long as it is slow and easy. Do this at least ten times, twice a day.

Relax all over

Lie on your back on the floor, arms comfortably by your side or resting on your hips. Wear loose, comfortable, warm clothes. You can't relax if you're shivering. Some people use a sleeping bag on cold days. If lying flat is uncomfortable for your lower back, try a cushion under your thighs, or lie on your side – a good position in later pregnancy. Keep the chin tucked in so that the back of the neck is long. Use a small cushion if necessary. If it is hard for you to get on and off the floor, sit in a comfortable chair.

There is no set routine for relaxation; some people like to start at the head, some at the feet. This is the pattern I prefer but you can alter it to suit you.

It's hard to relax if you keep having to refer to a book or think what to do next. If possible, make a cassette tape of the instructions – that's why I have written them out in the way I have. If your partner or a friend has a particularly soothing voice, ask them to make the tape for you. You could also have the instructions read to a background of soothing music which continues playing for ten or twenty minutes afterwards so that you can simply relax to the music. You can buy relaxation tapes from organizations listed in Reaching Out – see page 117. If you haven't got a tape recorder, you will find you soon become familiar with the routine and you can play some soft music while you relax.

Imagine you are in your favourite place – on a sunny beach perhaps, with the sea lapping gently against the shore, or lying on a green hillside in the countryside with the wind murmuring in the grass. Picture the scene in your mind. Feel the sun on your skin, the gentle breeze in your hair.

- Take a few slow, deep breaths, in through your nose, out through your mouth.
- Clench your toes tight ... tighter ... tighter still. Hold for a count of five ... and relax.
- Bend your feet back so that your toes point back towards your knees. Push hard ... harder ... harder still. Hold for a count of five ... and relax.
- Clench your calf muscles tight ... tighter ... tighter still. Hold for a count of five ... and relax.

13

- Tense your knees hard ... harder ... harder still. Hold for a count of five ... and relax.

- Tense your thigh muscles tight ... tighter ... tighter still. Hold for a count of five ... and relax.

- Clench your buttocks tight ... tighter ... tighter still. Hold for a count of five ... and relax.

- Press the small of your back into the floor. Press hard ... harder ... harder still. Hold for a count of five ... and relax.

- Place your hands below the rib-cage so that your finger-tips just touch, take a deep breath in through the nose pushing the fingertips apart as far as you can, then breathe out through the mouth. Again, breathe in ... and breath out. And again, breathe in ... and breathe out.

- Clench your fingers and hands into a tight fist. Clench them hard ... harder ... harder still. Hold it for a count of five ... and relax.

- Bend your arms at the elbows so that your forearms press against your upper arms hard ... harder ... harder still. Hold for a count of five ... and relax.

- Pull your shoulders backwards underneath you, as if trying to make your shoulder blades touch. Pull harder ... harder ... harder still. Hold for a count of five ... and relax.

- Now shrug your shoulders up towards your ears. Push them up as hard as you can ... harder ... harder still. Hold for a count of five ... and relax.

- Roll your head heavily from side to side three or four times.

- Clench your jaw together as hard as you can ... harder ... harder still. Hold for a count of five ... and relax.

- Wrinkle your nose into a sneer as hard as you can ... harder ... harder still. Hold for a count of five ... and relax.

- Screw your eyes up tight ... tighter ... tighter still. Hold for a count of five ... and relax.

● Now frown as hard as you can, frown really hard ... harder ... harder still. Hold for a count of five ... and relax.

● Now lie there in peace ... relax ... and just let go ...

Quick tension relief

Relaxing regularly like this will help you recognize when you are tense, so that you can learn when you *need* to relax. This will prevent you accumulating aches and pains, and will often clear a tension headache far more effectively than painkillers. It isn't always possible to lie down and go through an all-over body relaxation, but the following quick routine to ease tension in the neck and shoulders can be done even in a crowded office.

1 With your arms hanging loose and sitting up straight but relaxed, lift your shoulders up towards your ears as high as you can. Next pull your shoulders back and together, then pull your shoulders down as far as possible. Repeat the up, back, down movement several times.

2 Clasp your hands behind you, fingers intertwined, elbows bent. Press the upper arms in, squeezing the shoulder blades together. Repeat several times, breathing in deeply as you press back.

3 Sit with your hands on your thighs and your legs uncrossed. Drop your head slowly forwards, as far as it will go, tucking in your chin. When this is comfortable, do it with the weight of your arms added. Clasp your hands behind the top of your head and let your elbows fall forwards. *Don't* pull with them. Tuck in your chin and lower your head forwards until you feel the stretch down the back of your neck and spine. As this becomes comfortable, lower your head further, letting your back round. Hold, breathing deeply, then slowly uncurl, and lift your head.

4 With your head held straight and chin tucked in, clasp your hands behind the back of your head (your head, not your neck). Press your head back as hard as you can, pushing against it hard with your hands, then release the tension. Repeat several times.

15

5 Sit on your right hand to anchor the right shoulder, and tilt your head left until you feel the stretch down the right side of your neck. If this feels comfortable, add the weight of your left hand, not pulling but just resting it across the top of the head. Hold, then slowly lift the head. Repeat on the other side. Keep your chin tucked in throughout. You can also repeat this lowering your head diagonally forwards on each side, keeping the opposite hand tucked under you at the back of the chair.

Massage – shared relaxation
Massage is an excellent way to relax tense muscles and soothe tensions.

Few of us can afford professional massage and, in fact, some of the massage in beauty salons and health farms is of indifferent quality. If you are paying for massage, check what training the masseuse has had.

The best way is to learn the techniques ourselves along with our partner or a friend. Massage seems to have collected a sexual connotation, and it can be sexy if we want it to be. However, it can be purely friendly. Its advantage over relaxing alone is that touch is an important way of receiving and showing affection which we often neglect. That is another reason for learning massage ourselves – a professional can't put the same personal affection into their work.

Don't try massage with your partner or friend when you are out of sorts with one another. The underlying tension will be quickly picked up by the person receiving the massage.

Learn to massage the whole body, including head and face. It is soothing to have your back rubbed but the tension can simply move to another part of the body. A massage which omits the head can leave you with a splitting headache.

Massage is also relaxing for the person giving it. Even if you are the depressed one, don't let your partner or friend always be the one to give the massage. We all need care and attention. Alternate your roles as giver and receiver. If you are depressed, giving someone the pleasure of a caring massage may well lift your spirits and show you that you have something very worthwhile to give to others.

To explain massage takes a great deal of space and illustration. See the book list at the back for books on massage which are easy to understand and widely available. If you can't wait to try, here are a few guidelines for what can be at least a pleasurable way to share soothing touch.

You need a warm room, something firm but comfortable to lie on, such as a sleeping bag covered by a towel or old sheet, a small pillow for the head and some massage oil or lotion. Baby oil will do but if you use a lotion you need one that will not soak into the skin too quickly. It helps create the right atmosphere if you can turn the lights low and play soothing music.

You could start with the person receiving the massage lying on her back.

- Using your fingertips, start in the middle of the forehead, stroke lightly outwards, and then from the middle of the nose over the cheekbones, from the centre of the mouth, from the middle of the chin, and up under the jawline.

- With firm fingertip pressure, massage all over the partner's scalp, moving it over the skull in small circles.

- Ease tension in the neck by carefully rolling your partners head from side to side – make sure she lets *you* move her head and isn't making the movement herself. Working on one side at a time, reach your hand under her shoulder, fingers pointing away from you, then sweep your hand across towards the centre and up the back of her neck, ending with your fingertips in her hairline. Repeat several times each side.

- Massage her chest, using small circular strokes (but omit the breasts unless you are skilled), and massage the abdomen with large circles of your right hand *moving in a clockwise direction* (this is important as it's the direction of the intestine).

- Massage the arms, *always using firmer strokes towards the heart* – this applies in massaging all parts of the body where you do more than just lightly stroke the skin. Massage the hands using firm pressure of your fingertips and thumb, almost kneading the hands between them.

17

● Massage the fronts of the legs, *again towards the heart;* you can use small circular movements round the knees. Massage the feet in much the same way as the hands.

● Turn your partner over, and massage up the backs of the legs, over the ·buttocks and up the back. *Avoid any direct pressure on the spine.*

Meditation

Meditation relaxes the mind and heightens awareness of what you see, hear, touch, taste and smell. Practised regularly it leads to a more balanced personality and a reduction in stress symptoms. It can greatly help in depression and anxiety.

In a quiet room, sit or lie comfortably.

● Close your eyes.

● Relax all your muscles, beginning at the feet and progressing up to your face – see page 13.

● Breathe through your nose. Become aware of your breathing. As you breathe out say the word 'one' (or any other word of your choice that sounds calming to you) silently and slowly to yourself. Breathe easily and naturally. When distracting thoughts and worries come crowding into your mind, as they will at first, don't dwell on them but push them gently out of your mind and repeat 'one'.

● When you finish, don't stand up immediately. Sit or lie quietly for several minutes, first with your eyes closed, then open.

The whole process should take at least fifteen minutes. Do it at least once a day.

If you drop off to sleep while meditating, this defeats much of the purpose. Alter your position to one which is still relaxed but in which you're not so likely to nod off.

It helps to learn meditation with a teacher, at least at first. Meditation forms part of many religious practices and courses are sometimes advertised. Inquiries locally may unearth a teacher or classes, and see Reaching Out list. Before starting meditation with any teacher or organization, be clear about any financial transactions involved and the long-term aims of the group.

Yoga

Yoga is a physical and mental method of reducing stress. It starts with relaxation exercises followed by slow stretching exercises which increase body mobility and suppleness. It can be done at any age – my last yoga teacher was seventy. Don't be put off by pictures you may have seen of yogis in impossible positions. All good yoga teachers emphasize that you should not push yourself too far, and classes are graded according to ability. It's important to do it regularly if you are to benefit.

There are books on yoga but if you possibly can you should learn in a class. It is difficult otherwise to be sure that you are getting the positions exactly right, which is important. Yoga classes are common these days – and very popular – so it should be fairly easy to find one.

Coping with panic attacks

Panic attacks are the fight or flight mechanism working at full throttle, usually in situations which others would not expect to be alarming. That is not to say that they can't be absolutely terrifying. You may simply be setting off for the shops, then find yourself gripped by waves of nausea, your heart thudding, feel that you are struggling for breath. Those enduring this frightening experience often think that they may actually be going to die.

Panic attacks can occur when you are trying to ignore some stress in life, and are bottling up anxiety. The fear you are hiding breaks out at some unguarded moment and this can serve as a helpful signal to you to relax more, to discuss any worries with those involved or with someone close. However, if the panic attack is severe and you don't know the causes, you can develop a fear of the symptoms.

If you first experience a panic attack as you set off for the shops, the next time you go shopping you are already nervous that the same thing may happen again – which greatly increases the chances that it will. This can lead to you developing a phobia – a medical word for fear. Agoraphobia – fear of going out of the house and mixing with people – is common in women suffering from anxiety and depression. Some develop claustrophobia – a fear of enclosed spaces – others suffer from phobias about death, thunderstorms, spiders. It is possible to develop a phobia about almost anything.

Self-help can be very effective in overcoming a phobia, but it takes determination, especially at first.

It helps to know what is happening in your body during the panic attacks. Although the symptoms are alarming, they will pass, and they will pass more quickly if you accept them. Just tell yourself that you are not going to pass out or die, let the feelings wash over you and wait for them to pass. If you try to fight off the feelings of panic, you will release more adrenalin into your system and the panic symptoms will become worse.

You are far more likely to be able to overcome the attacks if you enlist the help of a trusted friend or relative. Confide your fears, explain how the panic attack feels and say that you need their assistance deliberately to expose yourself to the situation which frightens you, a little at a time.

If the problem is agoraphobia, for example, ask your helper simply to stand with you, holding your arm if you like, while you open the door and look out into the street. Let the feelings wash over you, breathe deeply – see page 12. Accept your fear and let it pass. The next day, take a few steps outside with your helper and stand there. The day after, try to take a few paces down the street, and so on. It can be done, and will become easier in time.

If you suffer from panic attacks and have developed a phobia which is limiting your life, do see what help your doctor can offer – he may refer you to a specialist. Also, I have listed organizations which help people suffering from phobias in Reaching Out – see page 118. Generally, however, we can treat phobias in very similar ways to other anxiety conditions and depression.

TWO

Love, Tears and Talking

There is no getting away from the fact that depression is to do with *feelings*, and we need to understand what affects our feelings in order to develop a plan to tackle depression. Why can one woman be widowed and steadily pick up the threads of normal life again, while another suffers a deep depression after her daughter has simply left home to go to college?

Virtually all depression follows some change involving loss (see page 8). What is important is what the loss *means* to us, its significance in our life. That is something that no-one else can judge and often we ourselves are unprepared for.

Molly was perplexed when she started to suffer from anxiety, depression and panic attacks after her married son moved house.

> If I think of visiting him I wake in the morning with my stomach churning and feel sick most of the day. It has completely upset my nerves and digestion.
>
> I had no trouble visiting him, his wife and children when he lived in Reading, and often used to stay with them. He is a doctor and the problem has only started since he was promoted to a hospital in Newcastle.

It emerged that Newcastle was connected with a sad episode in Molly's life, leading to the break-up of her marriage.

> We lived in Newcastle thirty years ago and for two years hardly a day went by that I was not in tears of despair. My mother-in-law was hateful – she was a very possessive mother – and we lived with my husband's sister who made my life a complete misery. So, with a three-month-old baby to look after, homesickness and all the other pressures piled on top, I eventually gave up and returned home to Southampton. We were divorced a year or so later.

As Mollie discovered, feelings that are not expressed can lie dormant within us for years and then take us aback by

21

the force with which they emerge. Our culture disapproves strongly of the expression of strong feelings. A newspaper headline following the death of a much-loved fim star, read: 'Stiff upper lip from sad sister'. The report spoke admiringly of how she 'bit her lip and blinked back the tears'. Two children orphaned in an accident were praised in the press for shedding barely a tear at their parents' funeral.

We all admire a brave spirit, and many of us would rather shed our tears in private. But the idea that it is wrong to cry has been taken to such lengths now that many of us feel ashamed to cry in front of our nearest and dearest, even ashamed to cry alone. We worry that we are not being brave, that we are letting the side down.

If we can't even cry at the death of someone we love, what were we given tears for?

Tears are a valuable physical release of sorrow and tension and part of the emotional healing process. If we don't allow ourselves to cry, we prevent natural healing from even getting under way. We lock the misery inside us, and that may lead to depression.

Grief is not an illness

It is important to accept that at some times during our lives all of us must expect to feel deeply unhappy, and need to cry. Grief is not an illness. If we have lost someone or something important to us, then the normal reaction is to feel sorrow, shed tears, want to talk about the loss. It is *abnormal* to carry on as though nothing has happened.

We are often quick to blame doctors who hand out tranquillizers as though they were happiness pills when the troubles lie far deeper, but doctors would be the first to admit that they cannot cure unhappiness. Sometimes it has to be borne, has to be given due measure as part of the human experience. If we take drugs to damp down these sad feelings, we risk halting the natural process of mourning and healing, stop ourselves from moving on, blank out the richness life still has to offer along with the sorrow.

One reason why people who are deeply unhappy may believe themselves to be ill, depressed, is that they are often unprepared for just how long a process mourning can be. This applies whether the loss is a death or the loss of something also important to us: a job, a home we loved, friends, a pet, our role as mother when our children leave home. It is very common for this process to take a full year or far longer.

Denial
First of all we may feel numb and shocked, we don't take in what has happened. Consciously or unconsciously we are saying, 'I can't believe it'. We may hear the person we have lost moving in the next room, still put out a cup for their tea, hear a dead child call out. If the loss is a relationship which has come to an end other than by death, we may think that if only we can be reunited, it will all be all right again.

Bargaining
We may try to bargain with Fate. 'If only I ... it won't really have happened, it will turn out to have been a mistake he will come back.' Usually, of course, it is hopeless.

Anger
Almost always after a loss we feel anger: anger that life could do this to us, that we could not prevent it, that the loved one left us. If it is a husband who has left us, all this anger may be focused on divorce proceedings and access to the children – which usually harms all concerned. If we have suffered bereavement, we still feel this anger at being left, at being so hurt, but we tend to deny it, because we know it is illogical. However, feelings are not logical. We may focus the anger on other relatives, or the hospital – why didn't they save our husband or child?

Depression
This stage of mourning can take a long time. We believe we should be getting over the loss but have a pervading feeling that the future is hopeless, we will never recover. This, too, is a natural stage of mourning, a sort of 'breathing space' the mind and body need before being ready to resume

normal life. It is important that we should still feel free to
talk about such feelings. It can be hard because relatives
and friends may believe that you should by now have got
over it, be pulling yourself together. It was someone to talk
to, someone who understood, that Pat missed most of all.

'My mother's death stirred up all sorts of feelings in me
besides the obvious grief. My mother-in-law, who had
died nine months previously, gave me more love than my
own mother, who was domineering. I had never been able
to do anything right for my mother. My father had died ten
years before. I loved the ground he walked on. I used to
stand at his grave and wish it was my mother in it and that
he was still alive. So when she did die I felt terribly guilty. It
was as if I had a heavy bar or iron over my head.'

At first Pat tried to deny her mother had died. 'I couldn't
cope with the funeral. I just went in and said "hello", not to
be rude, then went to the nearest motel and had a slap-up
meal. I sat there laughing with two sales reps and my
mother hadn't been buried fifty-five minutes. In the
supermarket somebody asked me how my mum was, and I
remember saying "Fine, thanks", even though she'd been
dead for three weeks. I didn't want to talk to anybody. I
carried on going to work.'

Gradually Pat became more and more depressed.

I used to walk around the streets after work. Although I had a
healthy son, I felt I had nothing to go home to. I used to sit in
tears some nights twisting my hands together. One night I
gripped so hard I made them bleed.

After a while I realized my mother wasn't here any more and
there was no more being the perfect daughter at her beck and
call. I just started to cry. I used to walk about like a zombie and
eat and eat and eat for comfort. I thought eating would solve
everything, but after eating I still felt empty. I put on three stone.

I didn't care about anything. I never made the bed, the
ironing piled up. For days I'd just sit in my chair. I'd still be
there in my dressing gown when my friend called in the afternoon. She used to tell me to pull myself together. Actually I like
to do housework, make the place look nice, but it's no use for
somebody who doesn't know how you feel to tell you to snap
out of it. You couldn't care less.

What I wanted was help. Not for people to feel sorry for me, but for someone to understand how I felt. I couldn't sleep, things were going through my mind the whole time, and I was just crying for someone to help me.

I had nobody to turn to. As good as my husband is, all he could say was, 'Go to the doctor', as if that would be a magic cure. It was as if he was in a tunnel; he didn't want to look to left or right.

Acceptance
If we have the inner resources and receive the right help, at last we do move on to the stage of acceptance. This doesn't mean that we don't still regret the loss, but we come to terms with it, again appreciate what life still has to offer, and begin to reshape our world.

Love, understanding and choice

What affects our inner resources, what makes us less or more able to withstand stress, to climb out of depression?

Generally, it will be the experiences of our early years. To some extent our ability to withstand depression will be affected by what we inherited genetically from our parents, but it is thought that our experiences while young are stronger than any possible genetic effect.

All human beings are born with three basic needs – for love, understanding and choice.[3]

When we feel loved and loving, we feel:
warmth, affectionate, happy, sexy, a sense of togetherness, belonging, closeness.

When we lack love or love has ended, we feel:
sad, rejected, lonely, lost, pain, a sense of longing, emptiness, fear.

When we understand and are understood, we feel:
valued, accepted, safe, relaxed, a sense of confidence, calm, self-esteem.

When we do not understand and believe others do not understand us, we feel:
anxious, lost, panicky, fearful, isolated, that life is meaningless.

When we feel that we can make choices, that we can direct our own life, we feel: powerful, strong, enthusiastic, fulfilled, a sense of energy, determination, satisfaction.	When we seem to have no choices, we feel: frustrated, helpless, resigned, impatient, a sense of irritation, fury, anger, depression.

Depression has been defined as the feeling that the self is worthless, the world is meaningless and the future hopeless – in other words, it is the denial of all three basic needs. How these needs were met when you were a child will affect how you feel today, how you cope with any new loss.

The death of a parent – for a woman particularly the loss of her mother before she was eleven – has been found to make us more liable to suffer from depression in adult life[4]. But it is not only those who lose a parent who may suffer an unfulfilled need for all-accepting love.

Many parents find it difficult, because of their own upbringing, to show affection warmly and openly. Their children can grow up craving warmth and affection which, when adult, may cause them to search for love desperately with the most unlikely people. This can lead to further rejection, further feelings of worthlessness.

Many parents, while believing that they are giving their children a good upbringing, tend to make them feel they are loved only so long as they behave the way the parents would like them to – love with strings. Notice how Pat said, 'I'd never been able to do anything right for my mother.'

Often behaviour is labelled 'bad' and punished when it is simply *child-like* behaviour. Can you remember being punished for some childish experiment – cutting your sister's hair, posting pennies through the floorboards, playing 'doctor's', trying all Mum's make-up? Children need to explore and are bound to make mistakes in their judgement, just like the young of any other species. If, as children, we were scolded for this sort of behaviour, we grow up feeling that there is something intrinsically wrong and unlovable about us – and that is not far enough for comfort from the depressed feeling of being worthless.

26

What went wrong?

One of the most crucial areas in which many of us feel we neither understand nor are understood, is marriage. We have extremely high – often unrealistically high – expectations of marriage. We believe that we are going to find a romance to last a lifetime, love, sexual fulfilment, friendship, support and sympathy when we're down, humour and pleasant companionship when we're up. Many of us, misled by romantic fiction, think that all it takes for a couple to meet each other's every need is 'true love'.

In reality successful marriage involves a great deal of very hard work, and uncomfortable if not painful readjustment. We would all agree that couples need to compromise, but we aren't prepared emotionally for the fact that compromise means *us* having to make concessions, too.

Some of our needs we shouldn't expect to fulfil inside marriage – most happily married couples agree that it is important to both of them to have separate friends and interests as well as those shared with their partner. This outside contact adds to the richness of the relationship.

If we haven't been effectively warned what hard work marriage is, nor helped to learn positive rather than destructive ways of communication with each other when there is conflict, we can all too quickly feel rejected and misunderstood, not knowing what is going wrong between us or what we can do about it.

Another gap between our expectations and the hand that life actually deals to us which can cause depression, is when our hopes of becoming a wife and/or mother are unfulfilled. Some of us wholeheartedly choose not to marry, not to have children. Like those who make an informed choice to be full-time wives and mothers, we may experience no regrets. But others find that marriage for them somehow never happens, the right person just doesn't seem to come along. Friends may say, 'I just don't understand why she never married.'

We may also regret not having children, particularly when our friends are starting families, or when we feel that our childbearing years are nearing an end. Few of us want to raise a child alone, so we may feel helpless to do anything about our childlessness. It seems so unfair.

Many married women – roughly one in ten – find that they are unable to have children with their partner. Many spend years undergoing tests and operations trying to conceive. There is a desperate need to understand – why me, why me? As the years tick by and the woman loses hope, she may become deeply depressed. Without a child, she may feel, life is meaningless.

ACTION PLAN

Grief denied can turn into depression, and we're more vulnerable to depression if we lack love and understanding, particularly if these needs were also unfulfilled when we were young.

Shed your tears

Crying is not a weakness. When you want to cry, cry! Sometimes it is inconvenient – at work or at the shops – so you choke back your tears. But don't think that because you have held back the tears that the grief has eased. You have simply driven your unhappiness further underground for a while. If you are to recover, if you are not to become or stay depressed, you need to find those tears again and shed them.

If you find it difficult to release your unhappiness as tears, but sit there instead with throbbing head, tensed muscles, bitterly miserable, try doing the deep breathing and relaxation exercises described on pages 12–15. Or ask a good friend or your partner to give you a massage. Easing the physical tension can allow the tears to flow, and release the feelings.

If your problem isn't to start crying but to stop, or at least ease up a little, your tears may well be masking another, to you even less acceptable, feeling such as anger. That's why the tears are not acting as the release you need. If you are stuck in that sort of helpless, 'I can't do anything about it' misery, see page 41.

Share your feelings

One of the greatest protections against depression is to be

able to share your feelings, to feel cared for and understood. Women who can confide in their husband or boyfriend have been found to be far less likely to suffer from depression after a major loss than those who confide in their mother, sister or friend. These in turn are less likely to suffer from depression than women who feel they have *no-one* to whom they can express their deepest feelings[4].

In our culture men are often taught from boyhood that it is unmanly to show feelings, or at least sorrow, tears and tenderness. This is partly why men's depression tends to show as physical symptoms such as heart and circulation problems or ulcers rather than by being openly unhappy.

If you are depressed and your partner won't (or possibly *can't*) talk to you about how you feel, try explaining that it is known to be important, that it will help, that it is not just self-indulgence on your part. If you can, persuade him to read this book.

If he still can't cope with you showing your feelings, or if your sorrow is actually because you have lost your partner, don't be too embarrassed or proud to confide in a friend, relative or neighbour. I was startled, when researching this book, to find how many women don't let even close friends know how low they're feeling. True, some may not react very helpfully, but you will have lost nothing, and from the one or two who can sit and let you pour out your heart, you will gain tremendous comfort and release.

Seek outside help

If you really have no-one to share your unhappiness and distress – or if despair hits you in the middle of the night when you don't like to disturb a friend – contact the Samaritans. They are rightly called the befrienders. You can talk to them face to face or simply pour out your unhappiness over the phone without even giving your name.

The Samaritans say they are 'the listening ear' and do not claim to provide treatment. But listening sympathetically is one of the best ways to help the depressed.

The death of your husband can be such a shattering blow that it is hard for those around you to understand just how devasted you feel and, of course, you have lost the very person with whom you may have been used to sharing your deepest emotions. After a few weeks even sympathetic friends may expect you to be back to normal when you still feel utterly crushed.

Even if you may be able to get through the day calmly you still need to pour out your feelings from time to time. If you have a widowed friend you will probably find that she understands how you feel better than anyone else. Do find out if there is a special group for widows meeting near you, such as Cruse. Sometimes they provide bereavement counselling and in any event you will find sympathy and understanding – see Reaching Out, page 119.

You might join a self-help group for people suffering from depression. Many women, like Pat, feel that husband, friends and neighbours don't sympathize, but discover that in a group they meet people who know just what they are going through, and it gives them a real opportunity to be open about their feelings. Self-help groups meet regularly to share their recent experiences over a cup of coffee and they will sometimes invite an outside speaker. Your doctor or the Samaritans will usually know if such a group meets near you, and some of the organizations listed in Reaching Out will be able to give you details of groups round the country.

Help to understand

Some of us may need more help than this. It may be that our burden of grief is so intolerable that we are indeed ill rather than unhappy, and should see a doctor. Unless your depression is purely the side-effect of another illness or medication, then you probably need help to understand better what lies behind it, because once you understand it, it is easier to tackle.

Doctors vary in how much they are able to help patients uncover the causes of their difficulties. Some make time to sit and talk with patients and give them a chance to unburden themselves. Some even offer psychotherapy or counselling. If your doctor has *not* had this training, ask him to refer you or suggest where you may obtain this help.

Psychotherapy

The essence of psychotherapy is that you talk, usually for an hour. The therapist does not pass judgements or tell you what to do. He will, however, help you to look afresh at your values, needs, hopes, fears, behaviour and judgement, and then to use your own new-found understanding to resolve your difficulties, anxieties and conflicts. You may see a psychotherapist for a few weeks or far longer. Some are medically trained, some not. This is largely irrelevant in psychotherapy. What matters is their skill in listening without making judgements and helping you to find your own solution rather than prescribing answers.

If you have a loving family and friends you may wonder, 'What's the point of talking to a psychotherapist, a stranger?' But part of the cause of many people's depression is their relationship with their partner or their family. Friends often cannot help giving advice, but what worked for them may not work for you. You are different people, with different childhood experiences. It is the psychotherapist's lack of involvement in your personal life, his ability not to make judgements about you or what you should do, that makes his help so often effective.

Jacqui saw a psychotherapist after her two-year-old son drowned.

After the funeral, I would go out in the car and drive it as fast as I could, hoping in a way to crash but not actually daring to do it. This went on for a year. My husband and I were still together – but only just. Eventually he suggested I needed treatment. On the surface I was apparently reasonably normal, but inside I was desperate.

I was always afraid of showing my feelings with my parents. They never had an argument in front of us, and if I did create trouble or shout I would be punished by silence from my mother. She would just shut me out for a few days, speak to my sister but not me. It crucified me, but as far as she was concerned it had a good effect because it brought me to heel.

I felt responsible for my son's death but I didn't talk about it to anyone. People were embarrassed about my son, and would cross the road to avoid talking to me. My mother has never mentioned him again. I've talked endlessly about it now to the

31

psychotherapist, but not really to anybody else. People say things like 'Don't be morbid' or 'Cheer up'. They want to jolly you out of it.

At first I thought the psychotherapist was ridiculous. She would remain silent until I spoke. It makes good sense to me now. You can say anything that comes into your head – I used to tell her about books I'd read, rows I'd had, anything, and she would find the most extraordinary things in it all.

Often she would point out that I was trying to say something to my mother. It all came to seem extremely sensible, and I stopped resisting. It was lovely. I discovered that I could see things intellectually quite easily, but the therapist said that wasn't the object, you've got to feel in *here*. Often when I got outside I'd be very tearful and I'd think 'Well, it's working, she's got to me'.

It changed me. I'm more serene. I cope better. I've got over my fear of upsetting my mother. I can talk about my feelings and I am able to deal with things without falling to pieces inside.

In many countries, there is only a limited amount of psychotherapy available through the health service and not that many psychotherapists in private practice.

If your doctor can't help you find a psychotherapist, you could contact one of the organizations listed in Reaching Out – see page 119. However, these organizations mostly refer you to psychotherapists in private practice and, while their fees are often modest compared with private medical treatment, they may be beyond your pocket.

Counselling is more widely available, and usually cheaper. Counsellors provide much the same type of non-judgemental, one-to-one, talking-it-through help as psychotherapists but it is likely to be less intensive. However, it is difficult to say whether one will be more helpful than the other. The quality and skill of the counsellor or psychotherapist you are seeing is more important than what they call themselves.

There are many different approaches but any good psychotherapist or counsellor will explain at your first interview what can be offered, what your agreement is about confidentiality, and what payment is involved – if any. He (or she) should be able to tell you where he or she goes regularly to scrutinize his own work and make it better. Very regular scrutiny of his work is important for you to be sure that there is little risk of a therapist or counsellor in fact working on his own problems through you, which could happen if he identified with some aspect of your situation – with you, your parents or your partner. He should also be able to make it clear what approach is brought to his work, in words you understand, otherwise he or she will be unable to help you. Don't be blinded by jargon – 'psycho-babble'.

The main source of counselling help in the UK is the National Marriage Guidance Council. Their counsellors – mostly women – are carefully selected and trained. Simply phone your local Marriage Guidance Council for an appointment. Most Marriage Guidance Councils ask you to make a contribution to costs but no-one is denied counselling because they cannot afford it. You don't have to be married to ask for their help, but if you have a partner, the counsellor may well suggest seeing him, too, as may a psychotherapist. Counselling services, or contacts for them, are listed in Reaching Out (Chapter 12).

You may luckily have a partner who will try anything if it will help lift your depression. However, he may be one of the many men who has a strong resistance to the idea of talking to anyone about his feelings. He may also feel that you are the one who's depressed, not him. 'There's nothing wrong with me,' he may say. Unfortunately, if he feels like this he is more likely to have been reluctant to talk to you about your feelings even in private at home.

If this is the case show him at least parts of this book, try to get over to him the fact that scientific studies have shown that women whose partners will talk to them about their innermost feelings suffer less from depression. If he finds it difficult to talk about his and your feelings, this is almost certainly a contributing factor to your depression, and you both need help to overcome this. Ask him just to give it a try – after all, what has he to lose?

If he is adamant that he won't go with you, don't give up the whole idea. You can still get valuable help from having counselling alone.

THREE

What's So Depressing About Being A Woman?

Men suffer from stress too, so why do twice as many women suffer from depression? Why do twice as many women take tranquillizers?

We all – men and women – need unconditional love, without strings. We need someone to confide in, someone to understand, and we need to understand the cause of our problems. Otherwise, we are vulnerable to depression. But we women are particularly vulnerable because of the way we look at ourselves and our feelings. Because of the roles we are expected to fulfil we often feel we have no choice or self-direction in our lives.

Yet healthy babies arrive in the world with a fierce urge to direct their lives. It is a kind of deep anger with the way things are that provides the energy to improve matters. Watch a baby learning to crawl. Her face reddens with fury as she tries to anchor that knee beneath her and push. This is *positive* anger, not the defensive anger we feel after being hurt or rejected. It is *drive* – the drive to walk, talk and feed herself.

Swallowed anger, dampened drive

We have this drive all our lives. But it can be frustrated. Little girls are often encouraged to curb their drive for independence very early in life. A mother is proud when someone calls her boy 'a forceful little lad'. It is recognition that he's an individual who stands up for what he wants; he'll be able to get on in the world. She may not be so proud if someone calls her little girl forceful. Girls aren't supposed to be like that.

Little girls soon learn that they should be sweet-natured, either giving way gracefully or getting what they want with charm or guile. They learn to suppress their drive and swallow their anger.

Why do they give up such a basic need? Above all, for love. Children will sacrifice anything for the sake of love and approval.

The lessons continue from babyhood to womanhood. Girls should be neater and quieter than boys; they should be content with the less demanding, poorer-paid jobs. To want more is to swim against the tide. While teenage boys openly rebel against their parents, teenage girls often face the impossible task of pleasing both boyfriend and parents. In the conflict they may lose sight of their own feelings altogether.

Career women may be dismissed as pushy, as freaks. Adult women are derided if they get angry. Male politicians can rage at each other and be admired as forceful men – such men have changed the world. But we don't like angry women. Female politicians know this, and accompany their strongest views with an ingratiating smile.

Angry women are shrews and nags; they are shrill; they scold; they look ugly when they're angry. Even 'I love you when you're angry' is a put-down. It shows the anger isn't taken seriously.

All this training to be quiet, selfless and ready to fit in to the demands of others takes its toll when something happens to make us unhappy.

Remember Penny, lonely and tearful in a new home in a strange area after her marriage to Graham? She said, 'My life was empty, totally empty. We'd talk it through and agree I had to get involved in this and that. But whenever I came up with a concrete suggestion, Graham would have a reason for my not pursuing it. He just doesn't like me going out, period. It's stupid, but he doesn't. I was angry and frustrated but I couldn't bring myself to say anything. I was probably frightened of his reaction.'

Keeping her anger bottled up put Penny under permanent stress. Depression has been called anger turned in on itself. Instead of letting it out, and possibly changing things, the anger is swallowed. But it doesn't go away.

Your unexpressed anger may manifest itself in a headache, a stiff neck, an aching back due to permanently tense muscles, stomach upsets, snappiness at trifles, tears – and depression. You may swing from wanting to lash out and tear down walls, to feeling helpless, powerless and hopeless.

Anger surfacing as depression can be traced back to childhood. We are scolded for anger, but tears are all right and bring comfort, so we learn to cry when we long to rage. This process has been called 'learned helplessness'.

Just as damaging is learned helpfulness, yet we learn it at our mothers' knee. Mother gives the best food to father and the children and puts herself last. Mother nurses father and the children through the flu even though she has flu herself. When an aged parent needs regular care, it is the daughter who provides it, or the son's wife. In a working couple, the wife still does most of the chores.

An angry voice inside may say 'What about me! Who's going to look after me!' But it usually gets repressed. A good woman, after all, doesn't think of herself.

Being able to stand up for ourselves leads to the twin traps of martyrdom and manipulation: 'They should show more gratitude after all I've done'.

Martyrdom is a sneaky way of getting power that we daren't take openly. Others sense it, resent it, and resist our demands. We soldier on, full of self-pity, and nobody appreciates us. And they won't, unless and until we are bold enough to say what we want. Then they can have the pleasure of giving, and earning our thanks.

Depression is sometimes a form of manipulation. It can be an unconscious attempt to get everyone else to run around us for a change. It works! We go on being depressed. We use depression to get our own way instead of saying what we want or don't want.

Many of us can't say no. We can't say no to the neighbour who wants a cup of tea at the wrong time; we can't turn down an invitation; we can't even say no to sex. A recent survey found that fifty per cent of married women sometimes have intercourse wishing they weren't.

You may be surprised to learn how often you martyr yourself. Take a pencil and paper and think back over the last few weeks. How many times have you sacrificed your own needs in favour of somebody else? You might like to do this with a friend.

Here are some examples from Mary and Elaine's list:

1 I found a cleaning job to pay for my son's driving lessons.

2 I had gastric flu but got up and cooked dinner for the family.

3 I went without new shoes and winter coat so the kids could have them instead, even though my shoes had worn through the sole.

4 I gave up my favourite TV show so my husband could watch what he wanted.

5 I let my own dinner get cold to make a meal for one of the kids who came in late.

6 I get up and feed and bath the baby and toddler before having a cup of tea and washing and dressing myself.

7 When I had a rare evening out, I left the dinner prepared, kids' pyjamas out, instructions on what to give them for supper and what time to put them to bed.

8 I went without meat for dinner so that the children and my husband could have it.

Of course there are times when it's right to put others' needs before our own – you don't quibble with a hurt child, for instance – but it should be a two-way traffic, especially with other adults. Now make a list of recent occasions when somebody else has put their needs aside in favour of yours. Which list is longer?

Confidence and cash

Being a wife and mother not only leads us to put ourselves in second place; it also can frustrate any hopes of free choice and independence. Before it happens, we look forward to motherhood through the rosiest of spectacles. We imagine the radiant mother cradling a gratefully gurgling baby while father looks fondly on.

Shirley did:

> I thought it would be beautiful. Our own house, a nice kitchen, and bathing the baby, putting him down in his pram, doing the housework, then going out shopping in the afternoon. But it didn't turn out like the dream.
>
> Nobody told me what to expect. The health visitor didn't tell me two-month-old babies don't sleep all night. I was worried sick. I thought there was something wrong with him, or me.

My husband didn't get involved. The first night we were at home with Andrew, I handed him over to Alan while I went to make a bottle. He ended up shouting that if I didn't come and get this screaming kid he'd sling him through the window.

Eighteen months later I had Graeme, and then we started to have money worries. People don't understand how tired you feel with two small children. I got so frustrated. Once I was coming downstairs with the baby in my arms and found Andrew on the potty in the middle of the stairs. I pushed him out of the way with my foot – not hard, but ages later he asked why I'd kicked him downstairs.

I was exhausted. Alan was putting in extra hours at work to ease our financial worries and got annoyed if he was woken, so I was running in and out of our bedroom, the baby's and Andrew's. One crying would wake the other.

The doctor gave me tranquillizers, but I still used to walk round the shops in tears, I was so depressed. In the end I took an overdose.

Looking back, I realize I was mad. I used to clean the house from top to bottom every day, but not any more. I have a friend now with small children and we often walk to the play area by the shops and sit there for a couple of hours. At least people come and talk to us, other mothers with small children.

If you are a mother at home with small children it is all too easy to become isolated. A job provides companions, but mothers at home – perhaps already anxious and insecure when motherhood doesn't live up to the dream – have to make an effort to find friends. Facing strangers may be frightening. Even catching a bus may become an impossible challenge. Everyday life becomes a tense, anxious ordeal, all confidence gone.

Parents teach boys to have self-confidence and to take on the world; they tend to protect little girls from it. Their experience of the world may be narrowed in childhood as it can be later by motherhood.

It helps to share feelings with a husband or partner, but many mothers can't. They may be single; or they may find that the strains of parenthood change the strongest relationship.

The man goes out to work, while the woman stays at

home with the children. He probably thinks she's got it easy – especially if he has a very tough, gruelling job. He doesn't want to come home from work and listen while she pours our her feelings. So she receives little understanding, sympathy and appreciation. Yet the self-esteem of mothers at home with small children often depends almost entirely on their husbands' attitudes.

Some men think that children are the woman's responsibility and expect to live the same life as they did before becoming a father.

Some women thrive on full-time motherhood and homecare. Others soon realize that they need work outside the home, at least part-time, to provide money and the company of other adults. Especially when there isn't a close, confiding relationship with her husband, a job can stop a woman becoming depressed. Women living in or near poverty who are prevented from working by their children are particularly prone to depression. Poor housing that might be tolerable if you are at work part of the day can seem like a prison if you're stuck there with very young children twenty-four hours a day.

Sandra lives in a high-rise flat with her three-year-old son Justin. Her husband left when Justin was eighteen months old.

I didn't want to live in a high-rise because Justin was so young, but the housing officer told me I'd have to be on the list for years for anything else. We're on the eleventh floor. It's noisy, windy, and there's nowhere for Justin to play. The week after we moved in he wet the bed night after night.

Living on welfare is degrading. I'd much rather work. I can't manage on the income. Last winter I couldn't afford heating, so I took Justin round and round the shops all day in his buggy. At least the warmth was free and it got me out of the flat.

I was desperate. At one point I remember standing on the balcony thinking that I wouldn't feel a thing if I went over the edge. Then I thought of Justin. I love him dearly and wouldn't change him but sometimes I look at him and think that if it wasn't for him I wouldn't have to live like this.

Eventually I got him into a nursery and applied for jobs – about seventy. Of the ones which asked whether you were married, single or had children, I didn't get a reply from ninety per cent. I've come to terms with it better now. But it's very depressing.

When last spoken to, Sandra was still looking for a job. All the talk of equal opportunities raised women's hopes, but in vain. Women are worse paid than men on all levels, and top jobs may be barred, particularly if they have children. Women who gave up careers to have children are often never able to get back on the career ladder.

Those who want work for company and self-confidence may give up the struggle, particularly if they are worried about the effect on the kids. In fact, there's no evidence that a working mother harms children at all, if there's good substitute care. But mothers have an automatic guilt button, regularly pressed by those who insist that a woman's place is in the home.

It's hard for a woman to feel confident when she is financially dependent on someone else. Relying on a husband's income, even willingly shared, makes it difficult to feel like an equal.

Some women feel they have lost part of themselves when they give up their job and independent income. Annette told me, 'Before I had the children I was an SRN and deputy matron. I didn't think of myself mainly as Derek's wife. But now I'm Derek's wife and Robert and Karen's mother. I go to the bakers' every day. Recently I went in alone. The lady served me and as I went out of the door she said, "Oh, it's you – I didn't recognize you without the children". That's happened several times. Now, when someone says, "Hello, you're Robert's mum", I say, "No, I'm Annette"'.

To have a job is to have individual status. To announce that you're a housewife and mother, supposedly a valued and honourable role in society, may sound less than glamorous. Mothers feel they count for little in today's world; many feel trapped and powerless.

Not only mothers suffer in this way. Single and married women may find themselves under pressure to give up their job and care for an aging parent. It's a woman's 'duty'.

Women who do so are at greater risk of suffering depression than mothers. Children grow up and make better companions as time goes by. Elderly parents can be cantankerous and demanding, and are likely to become more so. The daughter looking after them can easily forget she's an adult and allow herself to be dominated, replaying old scenes from childhood.

We tend to value people for the job they do and the money they earn. Anyone without a job risks losing self-confidence, feeling rejected, cut off from the mainstream of society, and helpless. As a mother said to me: 'You've only to look along the street to see which women have a job and which haven't. It shows in their step, in their faces as well as in their clothes.'

ACTION PLAN

Get in touch with your anger
If you feel stuck in your depression, if you have shed many tears but they bring no relief, see if your depression may be masking unexpressed anger. Try the following:

1 As soon as you get up in the morning look at yourself in the mirror. If someone else was looking at you, would they think you were depressed, or angry? Notice the set of your face and the way you hold your body.

2 Hunch your shoulders and hang your head. Close your eyes and think about how you feel.

3 If you feel flickers of anger, try saying 'Stop it' over and over again, louder and louder, or 'Get off my back' or 'I'd like to wring your neck'. What comes into your mind?

If incidents during the day make you tense and frustrated, try to release those feelings safely as soon as you can. You didn't shout at the shop assistant who, chatting to her friend, dawdled to serve you, leaving you frantically trying to stop two toddlers tugging at the display units. You lacked the nerve to tell your elderly Mum that tonight you were going to watch your choice on the TV not hers. Don't leave that damaging anger bottled up inside you. Release it! Punch a couple of pillows in your bedroom, shout in the bathroom, slam doors, strangle a towel, bite a cushion, dig the garden, knead bread, go for a run – whatever you like.

You may be surprised by the strength of feeling these techniques release in you. Don't be frightened. Letting your anger out like this can't hurt you or those dear to you – in fact, it will be less likely to come out in damaging ways once you are aware of what you are really feeling. Follow up with deep breathing and relaxation – see page 12.

When you get in touch with your anger like this you may find you are just thinking of an incident that irritated you that day, or you may find this widens out into more general anger about your situation. 'I shouldn't be left to look after the children by myself all over the weekend as well. I should be able to get out once in a while. That's typical of his selfish attitude. He never ...', and so on.

You may find yourself recalling incidents earlier in your life which made you feel just as upset and frustrated. 'It's just like when I was going to that party when I was a girl. My mother wouldn't let me choose what I was going to wear. She insisted on me wearing that old-fashioned formal dress and it made me look stupid. I was so embarrassed and awkward. She always seemed to muck up any chances I had of going out with people of my own age ...'

These thoughts are valuable pointers to what is behind your depression. Even if the incidents happened long ago they are still in your subconscious. The feelings aroused then are connected with the way you are feeling now. Bear them in mind as you move on to the next stage.

Look at your choices
You need pencil, paper and a couple of hours' peace and quiet for this. Draw up a list of the pressures contributing to your depression now. Diane's list read:

1 Father died a year ago and we were very close.

2 Mother has come to live with us and criticizes everything I do just as she did when I was a girl.

3 Frank, my husband, never sticks up for me, he hides behind his newspaper, or turns on the television. If I complain he says, 'There's no point in discussing it now.'

4 My daughter has a new job with a travel company, and a new boyfriend. She treats the house like a hotel, comes home at all hours, and I worry what they're up to. I moan at her, but now realize I'm jealous. I never had the chance to

learn languages and get a job like that – she may be going abroad next year.

5 We were going to move to a house where my mother could have had her own sitting room and leave us more privacy, but now they're cutting back at Frank's firm and we can't risk a larger mortgage.

Now go through your list and see what you cannot possibly change. Diane can't bring her father back to life. She can't be a teenage globetrotter. She can't create prosperity for her husband's company.

Neither can you single-handedly change society's attitude to women. But you can accept that you have suffered because of it. It is useful to understand that the pressures existed in your life because it stops you feeling to blame. There is little point in blaming anyone else, either – but your feelings are real. Accept them! Feel them! And let them go.

Life isn't fair. Some things we can't change. Once you've worked out what, accept that some things you have to live with. Other people are having an easier time than you, and others have it far worse. Cry for yourself when you need to. Direct your drive and anger to what you can change.

Go through your list again and see which pressures are the result of choices you made or shared. Some may be things you can't change. But if you see the part you played in creating a situation, you may see a more positive side to it.

Diane may feel that she has no choice but to put up with her mother. In fact, she and Frank could have left her where she was, living alone. But it was 300 miles away. Diane would have continually worried how her mother was managing. If anything had happened, and Diane wanted to look after her, she would have had to go to stay with her. It may help Diane cope with day-to-day irritations of life with her mother to remember that at least she is not tormented by guilt and anxiety. She and Frank did make a choice, the right one for them at the time.

Time for a change?
Next go through the list to see if and where you could make changes, tackle the situations differently.

It may demand simple direct action. Diane could find out what there is locally for people of her mother's age. If her mother could go to a drop-in centre or club a couple of times a week, it would give Diane valuable time alone to relax, or pursue her own interests.

She could learn French at evening classes and save for a trip to France in a couple of years.

If her mother can be left for a few hours, she could look for a part-time job which would give her an outside interest, company, and an independent income.

She could join a group or club which would mean an evening or two out each week, following her own interests rather than tailoring her life round her roles as wife, mother and caring daughter. She might decide that, while nothing can be done to alter the past, much can be done to try and alter the future for her and other women, or some particular group she feels gets a raw deal. It might help put her own problems in perspective, and working for a 'cause' could give her a feeling of power and achievement that she hasn't experienced in other areas of her life – see Reaching Out, page 120.

Making changes might mean learning to behave assertively, to deal with people as equals, without being either defensive or aggressive, so that her needs are given due consideration.

Diane could stop waiting for Frank to stick up for her – which is what her father used to do and partly why she misses him so much – and learn to stand up for herself.

Be assertive
To handle confrontation with confidence, it helps to have clear in your mind what you want to achieve, what you want to say.[3]

1 Pick your time and place. Don't open a conversation which you hope is going to result in important change just as the other person's favourite TV programme starts, or when they are about to go out.

Choose a time you know will be uninterrupted. If they then try to say it isn't convenient – which they may well do if they realize how determined you are – ask, 'When will be convenient then? This is important to me and I feel we will get on better if we have a proper talk. How about tomorrow morning over coffee?'

2 Describe specific behaviour, don't vaguely label the person. If Diane says to her mother, 'You're always nagging at me and treat me as if I'm six years old. You go on and on about how you used to do things but just stand and watch even when you could help', her mother will probably leap angrily to her own defence. Diane might say instead, 'Every time I have served dinner this week you have criticized the gravy.'

3 Acknowledge your feelings. Diane could add, 'I was hurt. I tried my best and I was unable to enjoy my meal afterwards.'

4 Say what you want changed. Again be specific. If you face people with blanket demands that they be more considerate, less selfish, less boring, they won't know where to start. Diane could say, 'I want you to make the gravy in future' or 'I want you to stop criticizing my cooking.'

5 Spell out the consequences. 'If you will not agree to this, Frank and I will eat separately.'

6 End on a positive note. 'I'm so glad we have talked openly about this. Now we will be able to relax over our meals together.'

Beware of red herrings the other person may throw in your path. Diane's mother might try, 'Every time we sit down to eat it reminds me of when I used to cook for your father.' Don't ignore what is said, or they will get more and more angry trying to get you to see their point. Acknowledge their feelings, but repeat your point. 'I do understand how upsetting that memory is for you, Mum, but I still want you to stop criticizing my cooking.'

Steer clear of history, too. As soon as one of you says 'You always ...' you are no longer talking about the particular behaviour you want changed. You are back into the history of your relationship – that cannot be changed but the future might.

Diane could use this technique to get Frank to wash up after dinner, to talk to her, with the television turned off, for half an hour after her mother has gone to bed, and to go out with her for an evening on their own once a week. She could use it to persuade her daughter to clean her own room regularly and always to let her know whether she will be home for dinner or not.

This is a very effective technique for changing the patterns of relationships that are troubling us, but do start with small steps. If Diane is honest with herself, she may be upset that Frank doesn't seem as loving towards her as he used to, and no longer much interested in her sexually, but that is a very risky subject for both of them. It is better left until Diane has confidence in her new assertive behaviour. (For more information on assertiveness techniques, see *Reaching Out*, page 119.)

Making such changes does take time, and you may find it a very hard struggle, particularly if you have been depressed for a while. If you feel defeated before you start, do look again at what I said about getting help – see pages 118–130. It can help if you take a friend into your confidence. You may well find that she is wanting to make changes too, and you can compare notes.

Keep reminding yourself that no matter how silly your feelings may appear to anyone else, you have a right to ask for what you want. Your wants are of equal value – no more, no less – to those of anyone else. There is absolutely no rule which says the needs of others must come before your own. Only put their needs first when you knowingly choose to do so. If you feel the need of further help, a psychotherapist or counsellor could help you look at your life, at what can be changed, and be supportive while you try.

If you feel you have cried enough, that what is needed now is to build up the impetus to start taking charge of your life again, but miserable negative thoughts keep dragging you down, a simple technique called 'blocking' can help. The idea is to substitute pleasant thoughts and images for depressing ones. For example, if Diane finds herself dissolving into tears over memories of her father at times when she wants to be up and doing, she could imagine him handing her a massive bunch of roses which burst into bloom as she takes them in her arms, obscuring everything else from view. All she can see are these beautiful vibrant flowers which represent her energy and passion, the beautiful things life still has in store for her.

Create a mental image that appeals to you and fits your purpose. Then, whenever you want to blot out troublesome thoughts, simply focus your mind and inner eye on this pleasant picture.

Of course, what I said before about expressing grief still holds good. You can't block out troublesome thoughts all the time. You may still regularly need to express your grief, too, but at times when you choose.

FOUR

Chemical Cures?

Most people suffering from anxiety and/or depression turn to their doctor, at some point. What many of them really need – and some know they want – is a listening ear and a sympathetic word.

Many doctors understand this and some put much time and energy into providing this support, but it can be hard for a GP with a busy practice to find time to draw out the patient's innermost feelings. Few doctors have had much training in counselling work, and some tend to take a 'pull your socks up' approach. Others, pressed for time and trained to think of illness in terms of bodily symptoms, automatically prescribe tranquillizers for women who complain of anxiety and depression.

Pat went to see her doctor a month after her mother died. 'I was just walking about shaking. I didn't care about anything. I never made the bed, the ironing piled up. He prescribed tablets. To him I was just a number, the 6.15 p.m. appointment and he had another at 6.20 p.m. – that's how quick it was. He was very nice but he was practically writing the prescription as I walked through the door.'

About forty million doses of tranquillizers are consumed round the world each day. In most Western countries including the United Kingdom, one in five women (and one in ten men) take tranquillizers at some time during the course of the year. To be fair, many doctors would prefer to take a different approach but most patients *expect* to walk away from the doctor's surgery with a prescription, something to make them better. So, how helpful are the drugs generally prescribed for depression and anxiety?

Minor tranquillizers

Minor tranquillizers are the most commonly prescribed mood-altering drugs. They relieve anxiety and relax tense

48

muscles. Reactive depression — see page 8 — is usually accompanied by anxiety, and minor tranquillizers can be a crutch to tide you over a particularly difficult time.

However, like all mood-altering drugs, tranquillizers do not *cure* depression or anxiety. They simply provide temporary relief from the symptoms. Self-help relaxation techniques can be as effective in the short-term and will be more help in the long run. There is also a risk that, by masking your true feelings, tranquillizers will lower your drive to face up to the real problem. And they tend to dull happy, positive emotions along with the unhappy ones.

The physical side-effects of minor tranquillizers, which can include dizziness, headache, blurred vision, are not usually much of a problem, as long as the tranquillizers are used for only a short period, but they can also affect alertness and performance at skilled work. Rarely, tranquillizers have what is called a paradoxical effect where the patient becomes agitated, excited and even violent.

The psychological side-effects can be more damaging. If every time something in life upsets us we reach for a bottle of tranquillizers we become less resilient, less able to take life as it comes, increasingly less prepared to cope with any serious crisis.

Tranquillizers can also seem to lower sexual desire and responsiveness, though loss of libido can be a symptom of depression so it is often difficult to know what is the real cause.

Minor tranquillizers are habit-forming. They lose their effectiveness against anxiety after four to six months of use, but many women take them for years, often on repeat prescriptions, without seeing their doctor. Most often they cause psychological dependence – you become frightened of facing life without the tranquillizers to take the edge off things. They can also be physically addictive and to stop using them can involve going through unpleasant withdrawal symptoms similar to those experienced on withdrawal from heroin and other hard drugs.

Stories like Angela's are too common.

I was on tranquillizers for fifteen years – ever since the break-up of my first marriage. After I remarried I thought I could cope with anything, do anything. It's only now I realize that I was just like a zombie. I was unpredictable in mood – and whether I was simply picking up the children or going to a wedding, I always had to have a pill first.

We moved eight years after our marriage. I tried to make an appointment to change my doctor. The receptionist asked if I was ill and I said I just wanted my tranquillizers. She told me to come in and collect my prescription. After that, I just phoned up. The doctor never saw me.

Then I changed my doctor again two years ago and the first question he asked me was why did I take tranquillizers. I had never thought – I had no answer. He said he'd give them to me for a month and then I'd have to see about stopping them. That was the big step.

I went through terrible withdrawal. I couldn't sleep, couldn't eat, was shaking from head to toe, had stomach cramps and my head was exploding. At one point I couldn't even get upstairs and my husband called the doctor. He treated me for a kidney infection, pumping me full of antibiotics – but it was just withdrawal, and he didn't realize.

I thought they would lock me up. I didn't want to sit indoors, but I had panic attacks if I tried to go out – it was horrible. I didn't care about myself, keeping myself clean, doing house-work, which I had always loved to do.

I had hallucinations. I'd see snakes crawling up behind the radiators in the lounge and big spiders running across the floor. I couldn't understand why nobody else noticed them, why the dog didn't chase them. I had a conversation with my dog one afternoon. I was sure he was talking to me. The wallpaper used to move.

Three months later I read about a woman who'd been through similar experiences, giving an address. I've never written a letter so quickly. She phoned me and I was so relieved to know that I was normal, that I wasn't going mad, and it would pass. If it hadn't been for that piece in the paper, I'd have cracked up.

It was horrific but I now know that withdrawal is better than staying on the drugs. The drug puts a barrier between you and the problem, so when you come off the drug you just have to face the problem again. With hypno-therapy [arranged through a self-help group] – really just deep relaxation and talking – I've now sorted out problems dating back to my childhood.

I've been off tranquillizers for eighteen months, and it's only in the last couple of months that I've felt really well. It's taken all that time. I can go out anywhere now. I'm a different person. The children notice it, everyone does. I can cope with almost any situation. It's so nice that I can manage on my own instead of throwing up my hands and saying, 'Help'. It really is a good feeling to know that I'm alive.

We were having lunch one Sunday recently and my twelve-year-old son said, 'Oh Mum, it is lovely to see you laugh.' I thought, 'You poor little devil, what have I put you through all this time?'

The severity of withdrawal symptoms can lead to doctors prescribing more tranquillizers. You may try to give them up, begin to feel absolutely ghastly – shaking, sweating, heart thumping – and go back to see your doctor within the week. His reaction may be that the tranquillizers must have been helping if you get into such a state without them, so he prescribes more.

But research has shown that the symptoms some people experience when they stop taking tranquillizers are not their original anxiety and depression returning. In double-blind trials, when people have not known whether they were taking tranquillizers or dummy tablets, it was those taking the tranquillizers who experienced withdrawal symptoms.

Major tranquillizers

When people are severely mentally disturbed, very anxious or agitated, suffering from hallucinations, and need a powerful sedative, they may be prescribed one of the major tranquillizers. These can bring great relief and enable many people who would otherwise be in mental hospitals to live near-normal lives at home.

Major tranquillizers are also used in small doses for the treatment of anxiety. If you have been prescribed one of them, regularly discuss with your doctor whether you still need them. Possible side-effects include stiffness of the neck and limbs, drowsiness and lethargy, weight gain and loss of sex drive. Also they can produce a feeling of indifference to life that can be extremely unpleasant.

Anti-depressants

These can relieve endogenous – see page 11 – but generally not reactive depression. Since eighty per cent of depression is reactive, the so-called anti-depressants are not miracle cures for all depressed people.

Tricyclic and tetracyclic anti-depressants

These are the most commonly prescribed anti-depressants. We don't know exactly how they work but it is thought they raise the levels of amines, the chemicals which affect our ability to react to pleasure and pain, in the body.

Side-effects such as faintness, blurred vision and sexual difficulties are felt by one in five patients as soon as they start taking the drugs, while the beneficial effect is often not felt for two to five weeks. Most people develop tolerance to the side-effects after one or two weeks, but if you are to take these anti-depressants it helps to be aware of the side-effects and, even so, you may need lots of support and reassurance from your doctor, family and friends. More than half the people prescribed anti-depressants either stop taking them before they have had a chance to work or take them in too small a dose.

Expect to continue taking a tricyclic for at least three weeks and possibly a few months. If you find the side-effects of one tricyclic intolerable, your doctor may prescribe another which suits you better, or perhaps a tetracyclic – the chemical structure differs slightly. Tell him, if any close relative has had good or bad experiences with particular drugs. Members of the same family often react similarly to drug treatments.

Once the drugs have helped correct the bio-chemical element in your depression, and lifted the black mood of despair, it's time to think about ending drug treatment. Tricyclics and tetracyclics are not addictive.

Like all mood-altering drugs, anti-depressants only treat the symptoms of depression, not the causes. To prevent your depression returning you almost certainly need to re-examine your way of life, attitudes and relationships – see page 21 onwards.

A few people may need to take anti-depressant drugs long-term, but not as many as are doing so. If you have been prescribed an anti-depressant, review with your doctor at least every three months whether you really need to keep taking the drug.

Mono-amine oxidase inhibitors (MAOIs)

Only three per cent of the drugs prescribed for depression are MAOIs. They have serious side-effects but they do seem to help a few people when other drugs can't. Like the tricyclic anti-depressants, they raise the levels of amines in the body, but in a different way: they block the process by which amines are broken down by enzymes. However, they block other enzymes and interfere with the way the body deals with a whole range of drugs – including the chemicals in some common foods, like cheese, Marmite, meat extracts and beans. The interaction of MAOIs and other chemicals can cause severe headaches, breathlessness, even brain haemorrhages and heart failure.

ECT (electro-convulsive therapy)

In the Thirties it was discovered that artificially induced fits helped lift severe depression in some patients. This is now achieved by passing an electric current through the brain – ECT. It is generally used for severely depressed people who don't respond to drug treatment. It is not a magic cure but it has helped severely depressed people to lead normal lives again.

It does cause some memory loss but this is usually recovered after the last treatment. When people complain of continuing memory loss it is thought that it is the continuing depression or anxiety that is producing the trouble and not the treatment itself.

But it is crucial to air your worries and, if you are not reassured, don't have ECT. If you are afraid it will cause you long-term damage, or are just generally anxious about it, it is less likely to help you.

ECT can be given as an in-patient or out-patient treatment. It usually takes about six treatments over two or three weeks to produce results. ECT works best on endogenous depression. It is not as useful for reactive depression, which means it is not helpful for the vast majority of depressed women.

There have been worries that some doctors may prescribe ECT too readily. If you, or a relative, have been prescribed ECT and are not happy about it, ask the doctor to explain to you why he feels it necessary. If you feel ECT should only be a 'last-resort', he may be able to prescribe alternative treatment.

However, severe depression is an extremely dangerous illness. Around twenty per cent of depressed patients try to commit suicide, and the doctor may be recommending ECT as a life-saving measure.

The only time you could be given ECT against your will is if you are compulsorily admitted to a psychiatric hospital or unit and the doctors feel it may save your life. This might be, for example, because you have tried to commit suicide, though ECT is far from generally prescribed even in these circumstances.

In all other circumstances you can refuse to have ECT just as you can refuse any other medical treatment, even if you are an in-patient. However, if you repeatedly refuse ECT and the doctors honestly feel they can do nothing else, they may ask you to leave the hospital or clinic and you have no right in law to demand to stay.

Over-the-counter drugs

Tranquillizers and anti-depressants are available in the UK, Australia, New Zealand and South Africa only with a doctor's prescription, but many women take other drugs sold over the counter to relieve symptoms of stress.

Pain relievers
Pain relievers, such as aspirin and paracetamol, are useful for the occasional ache and pain, particularly those connected with infection, but should not be taken regularly without a doctor's advice. Over-use can cause serious damage.

If you often suffer headaches or pains in other parts of your body, such as backache, talk to your doctor about possible causes, but also try relaxation techniques – see page 12. The way to ease aches brought on by tension is to relieve the tension, not simply dull pain-messages from the brain. Look at the problems that are causing your tension, to see if you can either alter them or react to them differently. I do worry about advertisements which suggest that women should use pain relievers for frequent tension headaches.

Remedies for indigestion and constipation
Don't regularly take remedies for indigestion or constipation without a doctor's advice. If you suffer from indigestion for more than a few days, or if it recurs at intervals, you may have a peptic ulcer.

Worry and stress can cause indigestion so, to ease or prevent this, learn relaxation techniques, try not to rush meals, and tackle the problems causing the stress.

Constipation can be linked with depression. You may worry that you are constipated, even when your system is working adequately, because you associate being regular with good health. It does not matter whether you go two or three times a day or two or three times a week. You should see your doctor if you develop a *change* in bowel habit, though if you go only a day or two over the normal for you, this is nothing to worry about.

Laxatives are only occasionally necessary, such as after childbirth and some operations. Using laxatives for a long time can lead to fluid, salt and fat loss, which may make you feel tired, weak and thirsty. Calcium loss may occur, leading to bone softening, and the bowel wall may become permanently damaged and inflamed.

If you worry about being constipated, eat more fruit and leafy vegetables, and add bran to your diet – see Chapter 5. Also, drink plenty of fluids, take regular exercise, and never ignore 'the call'. If you have already developed the habit of using laxatives, slowly reduce your dosage.

As with digestive problems, if stress, tension and anxiety or depression are linked with your worries about constipation, tackle those. Don't just fret about your bowels.

Alcohol

Increasing numbers of women are prescribing themselves alcohol to relieve depression and anxiety. It is one of the oldest tranquillizers but lulls the senses only for a short while. Though it does seem to act as a stimulant at first, it actually depresses brain activity, adding to the problem of depression, and bringing the risk of further serious problems. It is easy to become dependent on alcohol, and alcoholism is a disease which can shatter your life and the happiness of those who love you.

However, few of us want – or need – to avoid alcohol entirely. Moderate amounts can be beneficial, stimulating the digestion and encouraging relaxation. So what level of drinking counts as 'moderate'? What adds up to 'problem drinking'?

The maximum most women can drink without risk is four drinks a day, distributed throughout the day, not in just one sitting (for these purposes, a 'drink' is half a pint of beer or lager, a glass of table wine, a small glass of fortified wine like sherry or vermouth, or a pub measure of spirits). That means that three drinks is likely to be as much as you can safely consume in an evening, for example. You should try not to drink on more than four days a week.

If you are drinking more than this, try to cut down by, say, five drinks a week until you are down to the moderate level of a maximum of sixteen drinks in a week. If you are unable to do this, do seek help. Your family doctor will provide sympathy and support, and you can contact one of the special organizations to help those with alcohol problems listed in Reaching Out — see page 122.

Seeing the doctor

If you have been feeling anxious and/or depressed for a couple of weeks or more, do see your doctor, but go with realistic expectations. He is not a magician. If he confirms that you are suffering from 'depression', don't think, 'That's it, then. I'm ill. There's nothing I can do about it.' In fact, all the doctor may feel able to do is prescribe a drug to relieve some of the symptoms. The cause of the depression *you* will generally have to take further action to sort out.

If you are suffering from endogenous depression – see page 11 – anti-depressants may be very effective in raising your spirits within a few weeks, as long as you persevere with taking them and have been prescribed an appropriate dose – that's something to raise with your doctor.

If you are suffering from reactive depression – see page 8 – there is little a doctor can do other than listen sympathetically. Anti-depressants are unlikely to help. He may prescribe tranquillizers to ease your anxiety, but it's a good idea at least first to try the relaxation techniques described on page 12 to see if they help.

Many people accept a prescription for tranquillizers from their doctor and then don't take them. This is a waste, so do tell your doctor if you would like to try natural relaxation first. It is very hard for him to help you as well as he may be able if you are not honest with him.

Be sensible, too, about what you can expect. Your doctor cannot be friend and confidant to thousands of patients. If what you really need is someone to share your feelings with, consider whether a relative or friend might become closer if given the chance. When I raised the subject of depression among women I know, they found a lot of support simply through sharing their feelings, which they hadn't liked to do before.

If you can think of no-one you would want to confide in, the Samaritans will always provide a friendly listening ear – and you can usually talk to them face to face if you prefer that to talking on the telephone. If you need more help actually to work through your problems, then do look for counselling or psychotherapy – see page 29 onwards.

Your doctor can't make you happy if you have just suffered a terrible blow such as the loss of your husband. The grieving process is long and painful, but it is part of human experience. To dull yourself to the pain is to run the risk of not completing your mourning so that grief may re-emerge as more severe depression later in life.

Don't expect your doctor to be able to change your life. Pills are not the solution if your problem is that you have three children and live in a high-rise flat. You deserve sympathy – and hopefully he can give you this – but the way out of your depression is to decide which of your life circumstances you can change and work towards that end, at the same time learning to accept those things you cannot change.

Go prepared

- If this is the first time you are going to see your doctor about your depression or anxiety, make the appointment at a less busy time in the surgery – usually this will be in the afternoon. It is difficult for him to give you time and attention if there are twenty patients after you, and then he has a round of home visits.

- Take with you a note of all the symptoms that have been bothering you and of any problems and pressures that you think might be at least partly the cause. It is very easy otherwise to forget to mention what has been troubling you most.

- Tell your doctor about any over-the-counter drugs such as pain-relievers you take at all regularly. These might be causing side-effects, or cause problems if mixed with any drug he may prescribe.

- Take a note, too, of questions you want to raise. Here are some of the points you may wish to discuss.

1 Could your depression have a physical cause? Depression can be a side-effect of various drugs, of infections, of food allergy and other ailments. Tranquillizers and sympathy won't help if your problem is, for example, severe anaemia.

2 Is your depression probably reactive or endogenous?

3 Is there anything you can do to help yourself climb out of your depression?

4 If the doctor prescribes drug treatment, why has he chosen this particular drug, what type is it, what will it do, how soon will it take effect? Has it any side-effects?

- Write down his answers. He shouldn't resent it. Doctors know that most patients forget half of what has been said, not because they don't want to follow their doctor's advice but because they are tense and anxious, and no-one is very receptive in that state.

- Make sure you understand when and how to take any prescribed drugs. They are best kept out of your bedroom to avoid a possible mistake when you're drowsy. A good place is in a lockable cabinet out of reach of children.

- If you have definite physical symptoms such as aches or pains in particular parts of your body, persist in asking for them to be thoroughly checked out. Physical problems are sometimes overlooked by doctors who think that all the symptoms complained of must be associated with the depression and anxiety.

Once they have been checked out, however, if specialists have found no physical cause, be prepared to consider that the symptoms may be associated with your depression.

Grace was convinced she had multiple sclerosis. 'I felt detached and dizzy, as though my focus was out of joint. I was waking up at night with numb hands.' Her doctor carried out many tests, then referred her to a neurologist, who could find nothing wrong. 'All this went on for months. Every night, after putting the children to bed I'd collapse and cry because I was sure I wouldn't live to see them grow up.'

Grace had just had her second baby, closely followed by her husband falling ill with double pneumonia just after he'd set up in business on his own.

The baby was only five weeks old and our son then two. I thought having babies was easy and believed in getting back to normal life as quickly as possible. But I was rushing back and forth between the workshop and home, relaying instructions to the chap who worked for us – trying to keep him active – looking after my husband, Katie and John and doing all the chores as well.

Even so, my symptoms were so physical I was sure it was my body letting me down, I couldn't admit it was my head making me ill.

In the end I was reassured, though it took me two or three years not to think sometimes, 'Oh God, is it coming back?' Slowly I began to see that sometimes when I thought I wasn't worried, underneath I really was and would start watching myself for the symptoms to reappear.

I would think, 'My right foot's tingling'. I did go to another doctor once and we went through all the tests again. He told me that the human body can produce pretty strange symptoms which nine times out of ten are the result of stress and anxiety and nothing to do with any concealed disease. I believed him and, practically as I walked out of the surgery, the tingling went.

Some people find it hard to understand how closely the body can mirror the mind. If the problems causing your depression are very painful, or if you have a horror of the idea that you might have emotional problems, it may be more comfortable for you to believe that the problems are physical rather than face up to the emotional ones. Regular relaxation can prevent and relieve many stress-related symptoms such as headaches and backaches, but it may take more than this. If the problems are deeply rooted in your relationships past or present, then it is by looking at those that you will help yourself fell well again.

Breaking the habit

The following advice does not apply to someone who has just started to use tranquillizers, or just take a couple on bad days, and so is clearly not dependent.

Don't feel pressured into cutting down or stopping taking tranquillizers by anything you read – even in this book! – or by by what family or friends say. Unless *you* really feel ready to, trying to give up tranquillizers will probably cause you further problems. If you are sure you *want* to come off tranquillizers, here are some guidelines[5].

1 Tell you doctor that you want to come off, and work out a reduction programme together. It's important that doctors get feed-back about any problems with the treatments they offer.

2 If it's possible to explain the possible short-term reactions to your friends and family at the beginning, it will help. The more the people around you who can give support, the better. Many people have found that their families, like themselves, don't realize that the drugs are addictive – so when they have bad withdrawal effects they and their families think they are going slightly mad.

3 You may find that the best person to give you support is someone else who has been through withdrawal. You may also find that you have friends and acquaintances who have been on tranquillizers for years, once you start talking about it. Discovering that you are not alone in all of this, can make a lot of difference.

4 Don't assume that you are dependent. You may not be, and if you have used tranquillizers for only a few weeks you certainly won't be. People have very different experiences, and no-one knows how many longer-term users actually become dependent. But if you worry a lot about having withdrawal problems, the chances are you will have them. Keep an open mind, try it and see.

5 The hardest way to come off medication is to stop suddenly. If you have severe withdrawal symptoms, you may panic and go back on the full dosage. Then you will feel even more anxious and out of control.

6 With your doctor's guidance, wean yourself off *gradually*. If you go slowly, you can call a halt at any particular level, and stay there until you are ready to start reducing again – which may be many months. But you will have gained some confidence and control by having cut down a little.

7 On the other hand, most people don't want to be under this sort of stress for too long, and would rather get it over with. You may choose a shorter period if you feel you can do it. Reducing over about three weeks is probably as short as can be done. Lots of people will need to do it more slowly.

8 It may help to have your prescription changed to lower-dose tablets. Valium is made in 2 mg (milligram), 5 mg and 10 mg tablets. If you are taking three 5 mg tablets a day, you could change to six 2 mg tablets a day – two in the morning, two at lunchtime and two at night, reducing your intake from 15 mg to 12 mg. Then, choosing whatever time of day seems best, you could knock one tablet out – maybe at lunchtime. Then one of the breakfast ones, then one of the evening ones and so on. But do keep your doctor informed and don't rush the process against his advice.

9 Don't keep lowering, raising and lowering your dose if you feel you are dependent. Withdrawal symptoms are

worst when the level of tranquillizers in your blood is falling fastest. A smooth, gradual reduction will give you least problems.

10 Tranquillizers suppress dreaming sleep, and when people are coming off – apart from not being able to get sufficient sleep – they often have restless sleep with many dreams and nightmares. This can be seen as suppressed feelings coming back to light again, and your mind and emotions trying to work them through in your sleep. A sign of life!

We don't know enough about the psychological effects of taking tranquillizers for many years. We do know that they don't cure anxiety, but that they make you feel less anxious and more relaxed, at least for a while. It seems likely that many bad feelings get repressed by them, rather than simply going away. So part of what seems to happen for some people when they come off tranquillizers, is that they feel the need to start dealing with some of these things.

This can be difficult because our society generally frowns on people expressing fierce emotions – of joy, let alone anger or grief – which is partly why depression is so common. One of the aims of this book is to help you find a way other than tranquillizers to cope with your problems and feelings.

FIVE

Look After Yourself

Looking after our bodies can have startlingly good effects on our emotional well-being. An American psychologist gave one group of depressed patients psycho-analysis and took a second group running. The joggers showed more improvement. It raised their self-esteem and gave them a greater feeling of control over their lives.

Exercise benefits us in all sorts of ways. The fitter we are, the less liable we are to suffer ill-effects from stress. If we have had a row at work or with our husband, for example, that has left us all wound up, exercise will burn up the sugar and fat that stress released into our system. When we stop exercising, we feel relaxed and our body receives the trigger it needs to switch back 'to rest and digest'.

Vigorous exercise also releases into the bloodstream hormone-like substances which affect those vital brain amine levels, giving you a 'high' which helps you feel brighter, better able to concentrate. Exercise is Nature's anti-depressant pill!

What else can I say to try to convince you that taking more exercise is one of the best cures for depression and anxiety?

It will increase fitness and help you feel more lively if you simply start going for a brisk ten-minute walk every day. Walk to work or the shops instead of catching the bus, walk up the stairs instead of using the lift, buy an old bike and use that as much as you can instead of the bus or car. You can also release tensions by digging the garden (if it's been a bad day just think who you're sticking that spade into), or giving the floor a good scrub.

However, if you want really to attack your depression, releasing that 'high' which the American psychologist used to such good effect among his patients, you have to be rather more organised about exercising. This is true even if you're very unfit or getting on a bit. There are exercise classes now for the over-sixties. What is important is to find the safe level of exercise for you to start at, and then build up. Not having done anything energetic for twenty years is no excuse. I managed it – so can you!

First have a check-up

It is people who launch into vigorous exercise without a proper medical check-up and advice who figure in the heart-attack horror stories. *See your doctor before you start, and explain what you are intending to take on. Don't just assume that you are going to be all right.* This is especially important if you have ever suffered from heart disease or high blood pressure, have chest trouble, often feel faint or dizzy, have bone or joint problems such as arthritis, or have been ill recently.

Exercise needs to be vigorous enough to have a tonic effect, but not so extreme that your health is at risk. The way to make sure you don't take chances as you work towards your fitness is to learn how to check your pulse at your wrist, or neck (lay two fingers to one side of the Adam's apple).

Take your pulse first thing in the morning before it is increased by exertion, or even a cup of tea. Count the number of beats per minute (you can simply count the beats in ten seconds and multiply by six). The average for women is 75–90 beats a minute. If your pulse is in the 100s when you're sitting, lying or standing still, see your doctor straight away. If it's in the 90s your heart is having to work harder than it should to keep up with demand. As you get fitter, your resting pulse should come down.

Safe pulse rate

Take your pulse rate regularly during exercise to check if you're overdoing things – or not working hard enough. Don't stop during vigorous exercise to take your pulse – keep moving and take it quickly by the ten-second method to catch it before it falls. If your pulse is some way below your safe pulse rate, exercise more vigorously or you won't fully benefit.

If ever you feel pains in the chest, dizziness, feel sick, have stomach ache or digestive upsets, difficulty in breathing or a constricted chest, you may be overdoing things. Stop exercising and check with your doctor.

The maximum rate at which the heart can beat declines with age: from 200 beats a minute at age twenty to about 150 at age seventy. During exercise your pulse rate should reach but not rise above seventy-five per cent of your maximum. You also need to allow for being unfit, as follows.

To work out your safe pulse rate subtract your age from 200, then subtract a further handicap of forty for being unfit. A forty-year-old woman would get a safe pulse rate during exercise of 120 (200 − 40 − 40 = 120).

As you get fitter – you can tell partly by the way your resting pulse rate goes down — gradually reduce your fitness handicap, one beat at a time. As a rough guide, if you're under thirty you should be able to cut it out altogether. If you're aged thirty to forty you should be able to reduce it to about five. From forty-one to fifty get it down to fifteen. If you're over fifty, leave it at twenty.

Once our forty-year-old woman is fit, she should have a safe pulse rate during exercise of 150–155.

The sort of exercise you take should be of two types: bodywork and aerobic.

Bodywork

Your doctor should be able to suggest a ten- or twelve-minute routine of bodywork exercises to strengthen your muscles and keep you flexible. There are also many good books on exercising and in Reaching Out, page 120, I have listed a couple of these which are widely available. Regular yoga also accomplishes this, of course.

Aerobic exercise

Aerobics increase the body's ability to deliver blood (carrying the oxygen and nourishment needed for energy) to muscles and organs. For maximum benefit this vigorous form of exercise needs to be kept up for at least fifteen minutes, preferably twenty, at your safe pulse rate, three times a week.

Aerobic activities include brisk or uphill walking, jogging, running, cycling, skipping, energetic swimming, aerobics classes (as long as they are properly run by trained instructors) and some dance classes. Sports like golf are usually too gentle. Those like squash which involve short bursts of effort stress the heart too much over short periods.

It is aerobic activities, kept up for fifteen to twenty minutes minimum, which have the anti-depressant effect.

The benefit of joining an exercise or keep-fit class or swimming club is that the instructor should be able to help you gradually work up to fitness. Do check the qualifications of your instructor – badly taught aerobics can result in injuries.

An added bonus of joining a class is the company of classmates. Many women suffering from mild depression and anxiety are greatly helped by getting out of the home and meeting people. Getting fit provides a good opportunity.

If you are going to take up a sport, such as jogging, by yourself, the golden rule is to go gently. Just walk briskly for the first week, building up to half an hour's walking a day. The second week, walk for five minutes, jog for 15 seconds, walk for five minutes and so on. Then increase your jogs to thirty seconds and start to cut down the time spent walking in between – still start with five minutes walking, though. Over a couple of months gradually increase the jogging time and decrease the walking time until you are jogging for ten to twelve minutes at a stretch. Later you can slowly build up to jogging for fifteen to twenty minutes, checking your safe pulse rate regularly.

Again look for books about your chosen sport and see if there is a club in your area where you can get advice if need be. For example, you need to wear suitable running shoes with well cushioned soles, particularly at the heels, to prevent jarring.

Good food guide

Some women who are depressed almost stop bothering to eat at all. Others over-eat, tending also to eat foods which put on excess pounds, and that makes them feel even more miserable. When you are feeling tense or depressed, it can be extra hard to make the effort to organize a proper meal but if you fall into the habit of living out of the biscuit tin plus the odd slice of toast, you are going to add to your gloom and helplessness because you are depriving your body of the nutrients it needs in order to fight back.

If you are depressed or anxious, don't tackle overweight by going on a strict slimming diet. If you attempt a punishing diet that is beyond human endurance, you will fail – because it is natural to do so, not because you are at fault – but you will feel even more miserable and guilty. Also, many doctors now argue that strict dieting simply conditions the body to manage on less food, so that when we stop the diet we put pounds on again even though we are eating normally, not excessively.

Believing yourself to be overweight can just be a symptom of your depression. When we are depressed our self-esteem hits bottom. As women, we are encouraged to be over-conscious of our bodies and are surrounded by images of lithe beauty in advertisements, magazines and pin-up photos. This can lead us to focus our depression on our figure, blaming that for our problems when actually it is irrelevant.

If you are depressed *and* overweight, check with your doctor. Unless he considers that your overweight is a real threat to your health – if it is, he will advise you – forget about trying to diet at the moment. But *do* start exercising regularly. If you work up to three twenty-minute sessions a week of vigorous exercise at your safe pulse rate — see page 64 – the pepping-up effect on your metabolism will help your body to burn up food faster and you will lose weight while eating normally. And weight lost this way stays off, as long as you keep up the exercise.

While I don't recommend strict dieting to get slim, it certainly is important to eat healthily. This applies whether we are depressed or not, but is more likely to be overlooked when we are feeling low. It is another of these vicious circles – we don't eat properly because we feel depressed, and we feel more depressed because we aren't eating properly. Look after yourself – you deserve it.

You don't need to get involved in complicated cooking in

order to eat healthily – in fact, many foods are better for us eaten raw. Follow the traditional pattern of 'mains', filler, fruit and vegetables at mealtimes[6].

'Mains'	*A variety of these would provide*
Choose one of the following:	iron, calcium and other minerals, protein,
meat *	B vitamins
cheese *	
milk *	
eggs *	
poultry	*(Foods marked **
fish	*have a high fat*
beans and other pulses	*content.)*
nuts *	
Fillers	
bread	protein, B vitamins, some
rice	iron and calcium, fibre
pasta	(especially if whole grain
potatoes	cereals used and skins left
breakfast cereals	on potatoes). New potatoes are good source of vitamin C
Fruit and veg	
green vegetables, yellow/ red vegetables, fruit juices, citrus fruits, soft fruits (plums, pears)	Vitamin C, folic acid (a B vitamin important for blood), minerals, fibre, water

Try to eat three meals a day containing something from each list. Always eat a proper breakfast and, if you can, have your main meal mid-day so your body has a chance to burn it off.

High protein foods tend to make you more lively and to improve concentration. A high carbohydrate diet – sweet and starchy foods – tends to make you calmer, or positively lethargic.

A high protein breakfast helps get you off to a good bright start in the day but a half-pound steak half an hour before you go to bed isn't wise. If you are already rather tense, you may find a high-protein diet makes you nervous and generally over-stimulated, but anyone who is feeling tired, sluggish or irritable, with poor concentration mid-morning and after lunch, may find that cutting down on carbohydrates while upping their protein intake proves surprisingly helpful.

Don't go for long periods between meals. When you eat, your blood sugar level rises and then gradually falls again during the next few hours. If it falls low enough to reach its natural 'baseline', Nature's fail-safe control comes into action. Adrenalin is poured out to mobilize some of the sugar stored in the body and your blood sugar level rises again. However, this outpouring of adrenalin, which is the hormone that brings into play the fight or flight reaction, may also trigger off feelings of panic, tension, irritability.

You may very well be aware exactly when this moment arrives – I am. Don't push yourself to keep going. Stop, sit down, eat something. The temptation is to eat something sweet but, in fact, other foods raise the blood sugar level more effectively. If it's not time for a meal, eating a piece of fruit is a quick way of raising your blood sugar level, or a meat or cheese sandwich made with wholemeal bread is a healthy snack to tide you over.

If you feel generally tense and irritable, cut down the amount of coffee, tea and cocoa you drink, or substitute decaffeinated coffee, herbal teas and diluted fruit juices. A cup of coffee contains 100–200 mg caffeine, a cup of tea 50–100 mg, and cocoa 50–200 mg. Most of us are, in fact, dependent on daily doses of caffeine in tea and coffee. The effects vary from person to person but doses of 1,000 mg or more commonly produce restlessness, trembling, rapid beating of the heart, sleeping difficulties, ringing in the ears and flashes of light in front of the eyes.

Caffeine also increases the amount of acid in the stomach, so if you suffer from indigestion or stomach ulcers try to cut down your intake.

Targets to aim for in your eating patterns

Eat less fats

Cholesterol is the main ingredient of fatty deposits in the arteries and of gallstones. Our bodies make excess amounts when we eat too many high fat foods (the 'mains' marked with an asterisk have a high fat content). Below are suggestions for cutting down:

- Eat beans and other pulses instead of meat sometimes.
- Eat poultry (without the skin) and grilled fish rather than red meat.
- Cut the fat off meat.
- Don't put butter or margarine on vegetables.
- Spread butter or margarine only thinly on bread.
- Grill instead of frying foods.
- Substitute skimmed milk for ordinary milk.
- Cut right down on: cakes, pastries, biscuits, chocolates, sausages, salami.
- Eat less pork, lamb and cheese.

Eat less sugar

A high sugar intake encourages tooth decay, and only provides energy which we can obtain from other foods more healthily. We can become addicted to sugar, so over-eat sweet things and tend to become overweight. We don't need to eat *any* sugar, so:

- Cut down or out: sweets, cakes, biscuits, puddings, jams, soft drinks.
- Watch: labels on manufactured foods which will tell you what foods have sugar added to them.

Eat more fibre

A high-fibre diet is thought to protect us against many digestive ailments, and you can eat quite a lot of these foods without putting on excess pounds. Sizeable amounts provide the same energy as tiny amounts of sugar or fatty foods so it is harder to over-do them. Many of these foods are also good sources of proteins and several minerals and vitamins. Here are some suggestions for including more fibre in your diet:

- Eat more of the bulky foods listed in 'fillers'.
- Eat breakfast cereals made with the whole grain (not sugared ones).
- Switch to brown rice and pasta.
- Eat more wholemeal bread.
- Eat the skins of old potatoes as well as new ones.
- Eat a variety of fresh fruit and vegetables every day – raw whenever possible.

Changing our diet can be difficult because food means so much more to us than just fuel for our bodies. Our craving for food is closely bound up with our craving for love – we receive love and food together at our mother's breast and it is difficult for us to separate the two needs later in life. When we are so depressed that we cannot bother to feed ourselves, this mirrors our lack of self-love, our low opinion of ourselves.

If you find it difficult to change your eating patterns to more healthy ones, don't judge yourself harshly. It may take time. The guidelines given here are very much intended to be followed along with the other suggestions in the book for helping yourself to climb out of your depression. As you begin to do that, so you will find it easier to improve your eating habits. And this, in turn, will help you to recover more quickly from your depression.

Particularly if you are very overweight, it may help to think about what your weight means to you. Some of us carry round excess pounds as a shield against the world – though if anyone asked us we would say we long to lose weight. It is because we have a deep unconscious need of our extra pounds that we find it so hard to lose them. If you think this might be true of you, talk it through with your partner or a friend, in a group, with your doctor, counsellor or psychotherapist. You may find other ways to cope with your fears which are less of a health hazard.

If you think that it really is too much of an effort taking exercise, to change your eating habits, or if you are discouraged by the jeers of family or friends, just say to yourself, 'I am unique. There is no-one else like me in the world. If I don't take care of me, no-one else will.'

Set a routine

Even if you do not normally like to live to a routine, it can be very helpful if you are trying to pull yourself out of depression. The routine of life in a psychiatric ward is recognized as being a helpful part of the treatment – if nothing else, patients have to get up, get dressed and have breakfast by a set hour, eat regular meals, follow regular occupations.

If you are feeling really lethargic and tend to sit around in your dressing gown for hours in the morning, try writing yourself out a timetable for getting up, getting washed and dressed, putting on make-up – if you usually wear it – eating breakfast, exercising, shopping and so on. Writing it down may sound unnecessary but it can actually be less of an effort simply to do something by the time stated on a piece of paper every day than to find the willpower and impetus for each task afresh each time, especially if you can no longer see the purpose in anything much at all.

SIX

Sleep Soundly

Many depressed people are troubled by sleeplessness. If you suffer from reactive depression you may find it difficult to drop off at night, lie there tense and unhappy, and wake in the morning heavy-eyed and unrefreshed. If, on the other hand, you suffer from endogenous depression you will tend to wake in the early hours in a mood of black despair.

Feeling tired makes it harder to cope with the day, and sleeping difficulties can become one of the vicious circles of depression. You feel worse during the day because you haven't had a good night's sleep. You find it harder to sleep at night because you feel so low.

You may lie there thinking furiously and frustratedly, 'If only I could get a good night's sleep I know I would feel better tomorrow'. Mothers with young children, whose sleep is very likely to be interrupted, often feel desperately anxious to get off to sleep quickly in the evening but the more anxious they are to get off to sleep, the less they are able to do so.

So, how can you stop worrying? You won't come to any serious physical harm through lack of sleep. If you've always believed that you need a 'good eight hours a night' you may start worrying as soon as you sleep less than this. In fact, we all have very different needs for sleep. Some of us function well on five or six hours a night. As we get older we tend to need less sleep. Your body will not allow you to do without so much sleep that you actually come to harm through lack of it.

When you are finding it hard to drop off to sleep at night or waking in the small hours, you tend to underestimate how much sleep you have actually had. If you are finding it hard to sleep soundly because you are depressed or anxious, it is no wonder you find it so unpleasant and time drags. You go to bed hoping for oblivion from your worries and instead find them going round and round in your head.

If you follow up the other suggestions in this book about releasing your feelings, tackling the changes you can make and accepting what you can't change, eating healthily, taking exercise, learning to relax, these should all help you to sleep more easily. Here are some further suggestions, to help you during those dark hours of the night.

Think about the situations that can induce people to nod off during the day, even at times when they do not intend to sleep, such as driving down the motorway. Lack of sleep, food, boredom, security, familiarity, warmth and relaxation – all encourage sleep.

Lack of sleep seems obvious, but if you have had forty winks on the sofa during the evening, wake and then go to bed an hour later, that nap may be just enough, combined with your anxiety or depression, to make it hard for you to get off to sleep in bed. A short nap after lunch may be a good idea, if you have the opportunity, but if you cannot keep your eyes open during the evening, heed the natural promptings of your body and go to bed. It doesn't matter if that means you wake early. You can use the time for all sorts of useful purposes.

Help yourself to feel physically tired: tackle some tiring chores, go for a good long walk, dig the garden. Exercise and fresh air do make the eyelids droop.

It's difficult to sleep when you're hungry. It's not a good idea to have a heavy meal just before you go to bed because your body can make heavy weather of digesting it and that will keep you awake. But if by the end of the evening you feel a little hollow, a snack, with perhaps one of the traditional bedtime malted drinks, can help you sleep. Tea and coffee both contain stimulants, so avoid drinking them late in the evening.

A snack and a drink can be built into a bedtime routine that encourages sleepy boredom. Many people find that a little ritual of a snack, putting out the milk bottles, turning out the light, going upstairs, washing or having a bath, folding away their clothes, and reading for a few minutes provides an atmosphere of reassuring familiarity that helps them switch off.

I am a little wary of such rituals, however, because they can become compulsive. 'I can't sleep unless I've done so-and-so.' Routines are useful when we are going through a particularly difficult patch but when we feel better we should be able to get to sleep anywhere, anyhow. Think of mountaineers sleeping strapped together above sheer drops, and bargain hunters sleeping on the cold pavements outside department stores before the New Year sales.

Warmth is generally very important, however. A warm bath before you go to bed encourages sleepiness. Your bedroom should be warm, but not stuffy, and the bed should be comfortable. If you have a mattress like the Lost Valley and cannot afford to replace it put a couple of boards underneath. This will be beneficial for your back, too.

If you follow all these guidelines and still toss and turn, use the relaxation techniques described on page 13. If you have a tape-recorder you can make yourself a special bedtime tape. Emphasize feelings of warmth and sleepiness. After each time you say '... and relax' you can add 'and as I feel more and more relaxed, I feel warmer. I can feel the warmth going into my legs (or whatever) and I am feeling more and more comfortable. My eyes are getting tired and feeling heavier and heavier.'

At the end you can add 'and now I feel relaxed and warm all over. My eyes are so heavy I cannot keep them open. I feel drowsy and relaxed and I feel I must close my eyes. I am completely relaxed, warm and relaxed, comfortable all over, completely relaxed ...'

If you can't make a tape, it is possible to buy professionally made ones, or you can soon memorize a bedtime relaxation routine, since the very essence of it is that it is monotonous and repetitive.

If you tend to wake during the small hours or very early in the morning you may need to take a different approach.

If you wake in the night feeling tense, anxious and panicky, then the relaxation routine just described will help you. If, however, you wake in the night to a mood of black despair, and can see only unhappiness, then the best way to cope is to distract yourself by substituting pleasurable experiences for misery.

Don't just lie there listening to the clock ticking, watching shadows on the wall, desperately wishing yourself off to sleep and into oblivion from your black thoughts. If you know from experience that you won't just drop off again easily, accept this and make good use of the time.

Have a good book to read, waiting by the bed. Get up and have a drink and a snack if you feel like it. Knit or sew, if you enjoy it. Listen to soothing music. Is there something new you would like to learn? Use this time as bonus hours during which you can widen your horizons. Don't try to make any plans that involve worry but you could think what plants you would like to include in the garden next year, or plan a new colour scheme for a room.

After an hour or two you should feel drowsy again, and then you might use the relaxation routine to help you off to sleep.

If you wake feeling totally desolate, do get help. Wake someone in your family or even a friend. Obviously this isn't something you can do regularly, but during a crisis it is often essential. When Carol's husband left her, she woke a few times in a total black panic. She telephoned a friend who lived nearby and, having been through the same experience, knew how she felt. The friend didn't begrudge putting on a few clothes and coming round to Carol's house. She simply held her until the black moment had passed. Often, simply being held is the greatest comfort. Until we have asked, we don't know if someone is willing to provide it.

If there is no-one you can turn to, phone the Samaritans. They are ready to provide comfort day and night and know that the small hours are the black hours of the soul for many depressed people.

Sleeping pills

Sleeping pills *can* help someone in a crisis who is desperate for sleep. However, they are only effective in the same dosage for a few weeks, and if we continue to rely on them we are going to need an increased dose, which has obvious dangers. They are very habit-forming. If we carry on taking them for more than a month, then we have probably developed psychological dependence: we believe that the tablets are helping us sleep, and are scared of trying to go a night without them.

We also experience a slightly different quality of sleep when we take sleeping tablets. We have less REM (rapid eye-movement) sleep – the sleep during which we dream. It hasn't yet been established whether this is directly harmful but it seems unlikely that dreaming serves no purpose. And it has been found that when people stop taking sleeping tablets, they do extra dreaming – to make up for lost time, perhaps?

Sleeping pills have other dangers, too. Just before inducing sleep, they bring about a state of confusion. If they or any other tablets are by the bed, there is a risk that in the confused state you may take an extra dose, with possibly serious results. If you take sleeping tablets, do keep them out of the bedroom and well out of reach of children.

SEVEN

Good Sex is Good Medicine

Good sex can be the best tonic there is for someone suffering from anxiety and depression. Satisfying sex releases tensions, gives physical comfort and brings you close to another loving human being in a very special way. However, another of the vicious circles of depression is that it can lower sex-drive, even make sex seem repulsive.

Your sexual feelings cannot be separated from your other emotions. If you have a very low opinion of yourself, you probably don't rate yourself very highly sexually. If you are depressed, or finding it so hard to cope partly because your relationship with your partner is not very close or happy, then it stands to reason that your sexual relationship may be strained. Or, if you have just suffered a terrible blow, that may dampen down all your feelings for a while, including sexual desires.

If the earlier suggestions in this book help you to tackle your anxiety and depression, and the problems causing them, sexual interest should return. However, even when the depression lifts, you may find your sex drive unaccountably still seems low. The less you make love, the less you may feel like making love, and vice versa – up to a point! Stimulation of the erogenous areas of your body encourages production of hormones that make you feel sexy – and your levels may be low. So it helps to find a way you can start building up this hormone production – one that you can feel comfortable with.

This may involve discovering that you enjoy making love in different ways from your past pattern. It could be that one reason why your sex life has suffered when other pressures descended was that you were not finding it as pleasurable and satisfying as you hoped. Couples often have very fixed notions of the 'proper' way to make love. In fact, we are all differ sexually; what suits one may not please another.

One common factor that has been found to spoil women's enjoyment of sex is that their husband's idea of making love may not include enough kissing and cuddling to show his love and affection. Most women find it hard to enjoy sex unless they feel loved and desired and they can't be expected to realize this without being shown and told. Simply spending more time on tender wooing can transform many women's enjoyment of sex.

It also helps if you develop a deeper understanding of your own sexual nature. Most women would find the following exercises help to make their sexual relationships richer and more fulfilling, but they will be of particular value if you feel that sex has always been rather a disappointment. The exercises involve a voyage of discovery of one's own sexuality during which quite dramatic discoveries can be made, and what had been thought major problems solved.

To try them properly you need to set aside time each day when you can be relaxed, perhaps half an hour or an hour in the evening. Your first reaction may be, 'Oh, I can't do that. I have too much to do working, looking after my husband, the children and the house to spend an hour a day relaxing.' But an important part of discovering your full sexual nature is learning that you have a *right* to enjoyment in life, to please yourself, sometimes.

You may feel that exploring your own sexuality isn't 'nice', but it is a fundamental part of you. If you can learn to accept pleasure – in and out of bed – it can make your relationship with your partner richer and more mutually satisfying.

Also crucial to this sort of self-help is realization that as long as you try to please someone else in bed *all* the time you are not going to discover what really please *you*.

If you are happy with your sex life as it is, don't be pressured into feeling that there must be something wrong with it because of what someone else says. If you don't experience orgasm but feel satisfied, you have no problem and should not let anyone give you the idea that you have. On the other hand, if you don't climax and are left feeling frustrated, be prepared to discover that what will bring you to orgasm may not be what you or your partner expects.

Not every woman reaches orgasm through intercourse, for example, many climax through other forms of stimulation. Learn to accept pleasure wholeheartedly as well as give it, and learn to communicate openly what will give you pleasure.

I have set out this programme of discovery[7] in weeks, to give you some idea of the pace at which you might progress. Do not feel that you must treat this as a strict timetable, but resist the temptation to miss any stage out or hurry through faster because you think, 'I don't need to do that'. You could be subconsciously trying to omit or hurry through the very things that you most need to do. If you feel uncomfortable with some part of the work, persist until it *does* feel comfortable. Take two weeks rather than one; there's no rush.

Week One

1 In a warm room stand naked in front of a full-length mirror with the light on. Look at yourself carefully all over and then, looking at each part of your body in turn, tell yourself what you *like* about it. Too many of us grow up with a negative body image – we can endlessly list what is wrong with our bodies and never appreciate our good points. You may have a saggy bottom but have nice crinkle laughlines around your eyes. Perhaps your hair never holds a fashionable style but is soft to touch. Accept and like your body.

2 Two or three times this week take a leisurely bath, soap yourself sensuously all over. Caress your body, experiment with firm and light strokes, discover what feels good where. Dry yourself carefully and massage cream into your skin. Notice the different textures of the skin on different parts of your body.

3 Most days, give yourself time to relax – see page 12.

4 At least once, set aside time to do something that you find a treat – watch a favourite TV programme you often miss because of other commitments, settle down with a good book, have an afternoon snooze.

Good Sex is Good Medicine

Week Two

1 Sitting with your feet well apart and your knees bent, use a mirror to have a good look at your genitals. Then part the outer lips and you will see at the top the clitoris, in a fleshy hood. The clitoris is the most sensitive sexual organ in most women and stimulation of that or the area around it is what usually leads to orgasm. Below lie the inner lips, the urinary opening and beneath that the vaginal opening. Think about what you like about the look of your genitals.

2 Take baths and massage yourself as before, but this time also explore the feelings in the sexual parts of your body, your breasts, nipples and genitals (but don't massage your genitals with soap). Don't worry that you ought to be feeling anything specific, just discover what you *do* feel and what feels good. Experiment with different touches and movements.

3 Keep practising regular relaxation and add, or alternate, these pelvic exercises:

(a) Stand with your feet eighteen inches apart, heels flat on the ground. Press your fists into your back just above the waist. On an in-breath let your head fall back, keep breathing, and hold as long as comfortable. Then lift your head on an in-breath and on the out-breath let your head and top half of your body flop forwards like a rag doll, your fingertips dangling towards the ground. Stay in this position for a couple of minutes, then stand upright and relax. Repeat several times, keeping your heels firmly on the ground throughout.

(b) Lie on your back, arms by your side, palms to the floor, then draw up your knees until your feet are flat on the ground. Push up your bottom and arch your back so that both are off the ground. Hold and relax.

(c) Lie on your back, palms down and legs flat. On an in-breath arch your back, keeping your bottom on the ground and letting your pelvis fall in the direction of your feet. On an out-breath press your spine to the ground and lift your pelvis towards your head. Repeating these two movements as you breath in and out rocks the pelvis to and fro.

(d) Stand and rotate your hips in a circle like a hula dancer.

4 Say 'yes' to three things that you do want – for example, yes I want a biscuit, yes I want to leave the washing up till morning for once, yes I want to relax and read my book. Say 'no' to things you don't want to do. – I don't want to hump all the shopping around by myself, I don't want to be the one who picks up everybody's clothes from the floor. I don't want to be the one who takes the minutes at the PTA meeting yet again. You have a *right* to make these choices. Stick by them.

Week Three

1 Continue with body and genital massage and exploration. Don't expect orgasm but do keep on doing anything that feels good. Most women find it particularly pleasurable to massage the clitoris or area around it. Yes, this *is* masturbation. No, it *cannot* harm you, and is nothing to feel guilty about. Until you know how your body responds to stimulus and what you personally enjoy, you cannot help a partner to share your sexual pleasure. And when you have no partner present or want to enjoy sex without your partner, masturbation is the *natural* way to do it. Your sexual pleasure is yours – it is not something you have to give someone else, or that they can give to you without your participation.

2 Keep up the relaxation and pelvic exercises. Begin daily exercise of the muscles in the vaginal area, to improve sensation in the vagina.

(a) To find the vaginal muscles, try stopping the flow when you are urinating. Imagine that you have a drawstring pulling the vagina up towards the top of your head. Squeeze the muscles around the vagina for three seconds, then relax for three seconds. Repeat ten times, three times a day. Try not to clench the muscles around the anus, and if you are moving your stomach or buttock muscles then you are squeezing the wrong ones.

(b) Try to 'flutter' the vaginal muscles – this becomes easier with practice. Again, do this ten times, three times a day.

82

3 Think about what makes you anxious sexually, what makes you angry, and why. Try thinking through the situations beyond the point at which you normally cut off. What would actually happen if you let go? Would your partner really be shocked if you shouted with ecstasy? When you have the house to yourself, try shouting to see what it feels like. If you actually told your partner what you are angry about, might it not change things for the better? We tend to keep silent, even when things crucial for our happiness and the happiness of those around us are at stake.

4 Buy or borrow a good book on sex and read it.

Week Four

1 Keep up the body and genital massage.

2 Keep on with the relaxation, the pelvic exercises and the exercises for the vaginal muscles.

3 Try masturbating with a vibrator, if you like, particularly if manual masturbation hasn't by now brought you to climax.

4 List ten things that turn you on and ten things that turn you off. What are your favourite fantasies? Fantasy is one of the most effective sex-aids and it's free. Women often feel guilty about fantasizing but however wild your fantasies, you have no need to feel guilty. Fantasies are a very safe and practical way to add variety to your sex life.

Week Five

1 Continue with the leisurely sensuous baths, followed by massage and masturbation in whatever way you find most pleasurable. Try other ways. Devote enough time to it – if you want to reach orgasm and haven't yet, accept that it is usual for it to take half an hour or an hour of stimulation in these early stages. A vibrator can help.

2 Keep up all the exercises.

3 Give yourself at least an hour a week to do anything you like – even if it's simply putting your feet up and letting your mind go blank!

4 If you have a partner, begin to share your experience. A pleasant and easy way to start is to massage one another – see page 16. To avoid any sexual anxiety, agree beforehand that this will be massage for the pleasure it brings in itself, not as a prelude to sex. Massage is very enjoyable both for giver and receiver; it teaches us how to give and accept pleasure, and is healthily relaxing.

Week Six

1 Continue with the sensuous baths and masturbation. Because you are beginning to include your partner, don't feel that at this point your sexuality is a gift you must hand over. It is *yours* to enjoy.

2 Continue with the relaxation, pelvic and vaginal exercises.

3 Keep up the massage with your partner, beginning to touch the sexual areas, if you both feel comfortable doing that.

4 With your partner, each list the three things you would like to try that you feel would bring you greater pleasure when you make love. Talk about them, using words that come naturally to you – don't use medical words like penis and vagina if they sound odd, no-one else is going to hear you.

If you come up against real blocks when trying to follow these suggestions, do get expert help. Some GPs are able to advise on sexual problems, others have had little or no training in the subject. If your GP can't help, ask him to refer you to a specialist or sex therapist. Marriage Guidance Councils can also refer clients for sex therapy and I have included a list of contacts in Reaching Out – see page 125.

If you are taking drugs of any kind, check with your doctor whether they might be affecting your sex drive. Some mood-altering drugs prescribed for depression can have this effect (though it is difficult to know whether it is the depression or the drug, or a combination of the two that's lowering sex drive). Very rarely, the pill can affect sex drive. Don't just stop taking it – pregnancy can have a far more serious effect on your sex life! – but do talk to your doctor or family planning clinic about changing brands or method of contraception.

I end this chapter as I started – by stressing that sexual feelings cannot be separated from other emotions. Sex is one of many ways of communicating in a relationship. If your depression and anxiety are caused by a marriage that is unhappy on many fronts besides the sexual one, you will not be able to sort out the sex all by itself.

However, if you and your partner can improve general communication and understanding, the sexual self-help outlined here should improve and enrich that side of your life together. Equally, how you feel about your own sexuality is part of your view of yourself. Learning to be more understanding of your own sexual nature and needs can help you value yourself more highly, which is an important step away from depression.

EIGHT

It's That Time of the Month Again

Some women suffer from cyclic depression and anxiety. Anything from two days to two weeks before the start of their period they suffer many of the classic symptoms of depression and anxiety. Once their period starts, the mood lifts. Most women find that this pre-menstrual syndrome, popularly known as pre-menstrual tension (PMT) usually lasts the same number of days each month, but when they are suffering from other stresses and strains, PMT may last longer. In the same way, women who don't suffer from PMT may start to do so during a particularly difficult patch in their lives.

Hormone levels ebb and flow during each menstrual cycle. Some women seem to suffer from an extreme cycle while others only notice ill-effects when their resistance to life's stresses is fully stretched. It is certainly worth checking to see if your depression does run in cycles coinciding with your period, because that may require special treatment, but even if you are suffering from PMT, that does not negate everything said here about the causes of depression and anxiety and how we can tackle them. It would be unusual if PMT was the only cause of your depression. It is more likely to be one piece of the jigsaw.

Annette is obviously under various pressures:

I'd always been very casual, things didn't bother me at all. That is, until I came off the pill six months after our second child because it wasn't suiting me. I soon realized that for about a week before my period I was getting very tense, easily excitable and upset. I was taking it out on the children – they're three and one. The smallest thing made me leap and now, six months later, it's going on most of the time really.

I have a break from it for a few days during my period and perhaps a few days after, then it begins again.

It starts very gradually, then I find myself screeching at the children and I think 'Here we go again'. It's not like me. I feel guilty. I hear myself saying hateful things, not just shouting but being horrid with it.

I've been rowing with my husband for six months now. I keep a lot of my problems to myself, and the most aggravating thing was when he used to say, 'Wrong time of the month?' It infuriated me. He's stopped saying it because I got so furious.

It's hard to cope with having two children so close together – there's only fourteen months between them. It's not just being bad-tempered but the tiredness that gets me down. I get up in the morning tired. If I sit down in the afternoon I'm asleep instantly, but not for more than a couple of minutes because Christopher will say 'Mummy', and wake me up.

I'm good at covering up. I can be very bad-tempered and irritable and somebody can come to the door and I snap out of it instantly. I'm not a great one for telling everyone how I'm feeling.

I do miss work, especially the company. I'm sure that if I was at work I'd hardly notice the PMT because there'd be too much to occupy me. I think most illness is less if you're at work. If I get a heavy cold now I'm aware of it, but I used to go to work with a heavy cold and not take any notice of it.

The worst of being just a mum – I shouldn't say *just* a mum – is that you lose your identity. All my friends now are made through the children. I make an effort to keep up friendships with two women who were at ante-natal classes with me. We take turns to have lunch with each other. One of them gets very depressed – PMT, like me – since the birth of her second child.

When I start snapping I'm absolutely dreadful. Christopher wanted to help me polish the television so I sprayed it for him. He was polishing it and I shouted 'and the bottom half', instead of saying 'you haven't done this bit down here'. I hate myself the minute I open my mouth.

How can you tell whether you are suffering from PMT? Many of the symptoms – headaches, irritability, difficulty concentrating – are the same as in other forms of depression or anxiety states. Particular symptoms of PMT are weight gain during those few days, painful breasts and feeling bloated. If you *are* suffering from PMT, your depression and anxiety will increase noticeably during the days before your period.

A woman's menstrual cycle is largely controlled by the ebb and flow of two hormones, oestrogen and progesterone. An alteration to their balance can have a strong effect on the way other hormones do their job in the body. PMT is often associated with high levels of oestrogen and low levels of progesterone. It is now believed by many doctors that the cause of the trouble, the reason why the hormones are out of balance, is a shortage in the body of substances called essential fatty acids, EFAs.

If you think you may be suffering from PMT, keep a daily chart for three months, noting any symptoms you experience, and the duration of your period. Take this along when you consult your doctor as it will help him to treat you.

He may try various treatments. For fairly mild cases, diuretics, which make you urinate more frequently, can relieve bloatedness and help you feel better generally.

Vitamin B6 (pyridoxine) may help, taken daily for some days before the expected start of symptoms until a few days after the start of the period. Pyridoxine increases the efficiency with which the body tissues make use of EFAs.

Evening primrose oil (Efamol) has had impressive results and it's worth asking your doctor about trying this. It is believed to correct the underlying deficiency of EFAs.

Hormonal treatment can include going on the pill, if it's suitable for you, to change the oestrogen-progesterone balance. Other women are helped by treatment to replace the missing progesterone. Because this is altered when it passes through the digestive system, it is given in the form of pessaries to be inserted in the vagina, or suppositories to be inserted in the rectum. In very severe cases progesterone may be given by injection. This is an expensive method, but preferred by many women who don't like using pessaries or suppositories. Progestogen, a synthetic hormone that can be taken orally, helps some women but makes others feel worse.

If you think that your depression may be due even in part to PMT do seek treatment. The longer you suffer from it, the worse it gets. However, not all doctors are as informed or sympathetic as they might be about PMT. If yours falls into this category, contact one of the organizations listed in Reaching Out – see page 120.

Do also try the other methods of self-help suggested. Relaxation and exercise can certainly help relieve tension. On those days when you are particularly liable to be short-tempered, don't leave too long an interval between meals, because this can lead to a fall in your blood-sugar level and increased irritability.

NINE

Childbirth and Depression

In one city area half the mothers with pre-school children were found to suffer from moderate to severe depression during just one year. For many, many women starting a family fits into place the last piece of their jigsaw of depression. We have already looked at many of the special pressures on women at this time. However, there can be an extra factor contributing to the depression suffered by about one in ten mothers after childbirth – a hormonal one.

During pregnancy the placenta (where the baby's umbilical cord joins the womb, taking nourishment and returning waste to the mother's system) becomes a virtual hormone factory, producing large amounts of oestrogen and progesterone. Progesterone levels in the body can rise up to thirty times higher than the normal peak level of progesterone during the menstrual cycle. Progesterone has a calming effect on the body and is thought to be one reason why women feel so placid and cow-like during pregnancy.

When the baby and placenta are delivered, this supply of hormones is suddenly cut off. It has taken months to build up the high levels of oestrogen and progesterone but within hours there may be virtually none.

The 'baby blues', the weepiness which affects about fifty per cent of all new mothers, is now generally accepted to be one result of this sudden fall in hormone levels, but it is not full-blooded postnatal depression. It usually affects mothers three to five days after the birth, though it can start on the first day. Crying spells can be triggered by any little upset or seemingly by sheer happiness. Those who are breast-feeding often burst into tears over any feeding difficulty, however small. Mothers suffering from baby blues also tend to be very touchy and have poor concentration.

Very rarely the blues may last a month or so but usually they are over by the tenth day.

Postnatal depression is far more serious and longer lasting but this, too, may be triggered by changes in hormone levels.

Some women suffering from severe postnatal depression have been helped by treatment with progesterone. After childbirth there is little progesterone in the body until two weeks before the first period, when the woman's menstrual cycle is re-establishing itself. Even then, progesterone isn't present in anything like the same quantities as during pregnancy. Different placentas produce differing amounts of progesterone, so some women have to adapt to more extreme changes than others. Also, some probably find it harder to adapt to the lack of progesterone – and their ability to adapt will be affected by other stresses in their lives.

Postnatal depression may start soon after the birth – almost a continuation of the baby blues – or it can start a few weeks or months afterwards. The depression may end with the first period or it may emerge as pre-menstrual tension once the woman's periods are re-established. Sometimes it starts when the mother resumes taking an oral contraceptive pill, especially the progestogen-only type (the mini-pill). Progestogens may lower the blood progesterone level.

How can we tell if a depression may be associated with low progesterone levels and may therefore be helped by progesterone treatment?

With this type of postnatal depression you are nearly always thirsty and hungry, and tend to crave fattening carbohydrate foods such as sweets and biscuits. Within a month or two you may be as heavy as you were just before the baby was born. You will usually be very irritable and tend to feel worse as the day goes on.

While people with either reactive or endogenous depression usually have sleeping problems — difficulty getting off to sleep, sleeping fitfully or waking early — women with postnatal depression usually yearn for sleep and seem never to get enough. They sleep heavily, but wake instantly if the baby wakes. This longing to sleep as soon as their head hits the pillow can also place an additional strain on their sex life.

Ellie suffered from severe postnatal depression.

It's difficult to define when I started feeling really depressed. I was always tired, I never caught up, and every day accumulated the tiredness.

The birth was induced and a forceps delivery, which left me exhausted. I was sleepy with injections and they took Matthew away after the birth. I wanted him to stay with me. After a couple of days I wanted to get out of hospital as quickly as possible, I didn't like the atmosphere or the routine. I had the baby blues. I was crying over feeding problems – I thought there was something wrong with Matthew. They didn't tell me feeding would take up so much time. I think they gave him a bottle at night, which I didn't like, but I was so exhausted I accepted it.

They told me the baby blues would last only a couple of days so I didn't worry overmuch. There were one or two days like that over the next month or so, but nothing traumatic.

When I left hospital, I still had trouble feeding him. When mothers or the midwife came to see me I would write down everything they told me, in case I forgot. I was obsessive about doing everything right. I was totally different to the woman I was before I had the baby.

I felt worse and worse. I talked to the health visitor and the midwife. They said I'd feel better in six weeks, then another six weeks, that I had postnatal depression. But it didn't go away. I was totally exhausted. Even thinking about cooking a meal was an enormous effort, just impossible.

We had moved to a new house in the country a couple of months before Matthew was born. I had no car, no neighbours, nobody around to talk to about the things that can go wrong with a baby.

One afternoon I took an overdose. I put the baby to bed, and I felt absolutely exhausted. The doctor had given me tranquillizers, and I took some, feeling I just wanted a good long sleep. Before I was really drowsy I realized I had done something wrong, so I phoned the health visitor.

After that, everybody realized there must be something seriously wrong. I began to see a specialist and he started me on anti-depressants. I didn't get any better, but from then on I felt I had to fight something inside myself – it was as if there were two sides to me and I was fighting the other side. If I didn't keep it down it would take me over.

Childbirth and Depression

I would freak out. I wanted to take my clothes off and run across the fields. I wanted to push my fists through a glass pane, and my husband had to stop me. All the time I had to fight down a desire to break out, to do extreme, dramatic things. Chris isn't the sort to talk about feelings and I suppose I was trying to make him understand how desperate I was. I felt held down and controlled – I guess by the baby.

Chris encouraged me to do constructive things like painting, but I couldn't get it together. I did do the garden – I dug a huge vegetable plot. I just went on digging, digging, digging until 10 o'clock at night so that I could make myself physically feel as if I'd done something. I remember planting four blackberry bushes. Chris thought I was mad. I just stayed out there getting soaking wet in the pouring rain moving those bushes, just so I could feel something. I could feel the rain and I could feel I was doing something different from just cleaning and feeding the baby.

Two months after the first overdose I did it again. At that point I think I did want to die. I was unconscious for a couple of days. I didn't see any way out of the situation I was in and it seemed the most sensible thing to do.

I thought I must be really mad. Nobody seemed to understand me and I felt they were all controlling me. I couldn't even manage to stop breast-feeding when I wanted to. I felt it was part of what was dragging me down but everyone said I shouldn't stop – husband, mother, mother-in-law. I wasn't strong enough, I didn't have a mind of my own – I didn't feel I had enough power in myself to do what I wanted to do, whereas all the time before, when I was working, I had.

Gradually I started to feel a bit better and reduce the dose of anti-depressants. When Matthew was 1½ I finally stopped taking them.

I really missed out on all the baby side of Matthew. My mother and mother-in-law helped look after him. I can't remember enjoying any part of him while he was a baby. I am probably over protective of him now.

Once I was out of the depression, I thought 'Right, I must organize my life'. I wanted to be able to talk to people in the village two miles away. I got a car – we couldn't afford it, but it was a necessity. I went to the toddlers' group. That was difficult but I pushed myself, and in the end I took it over and started running it. That was great for me because it gave me something I

93

could do besides looking after Matthew. I started to get more sociable, met other mums, go round for coffee. It went on from there.

I think we should be more informed, more prepared. None of the books on pregnancy and childcare I ever read went further than saying you might have two or three days when you want to cry. I should have thought there should be a sizeable chapter on postnatal depression. That would have helped me. It might not have prevented it happening but it would have helped me understand.

Another type of postnatal depression can occur after the mother stops breast-feeding, due to a high level of prolactin in the blood. One of the many functions of prolactin is to prepare the breasts for milk production and then to stimulate the supply of milk once the mother is feeding. When she stops breast-feeding the prolactin level should return to that of a non-pregnant woman. If it doesn't, she may suffer from depression. One sign that this may be the problem is that there may still be milk in the breasts two months or more after she has finished breast-feeding.

ACTION PLAN

Many of the suggestions already made in this book will apply to you if you're suffering from postnatal depression and I won't repeat them all here. However, do check with your doctor whether your depression may have a hormonal element. Discuss with him the details of when you started feeling depressed and the exact symptoms. He may arrange a blood test to discover the level of progesterone, and of prolactin if you have finished breast-feeding. He may also test for other deficiencies, such as anaemia. He may prescribe progesterone treatment, probably in the form of pessaries or suppositories.

Some doctors, however, are very wary of hormone treatments. There is disagreement in the medical profession as to whether postnatal depression is directly linked with low levels of progesterone, though there is mounting evidence that there is a connection. Some women with postnatal depression have been helped by progesterone treatment.

If your doctor is reluctant to consider this treatment and you want to try, you could point out that progesterone has been found to be very safe in treatment over many years, it aids breast-feeding, and there is no risk that a patient can overdose on progesterone suppositories as can be done with anti-depressants.

What is particularly cheering about progesterone treatment is that it may be used as a preventive measure. After one serious bout of postnatal depression many women (and their husbands) are very worried about having another child. If progesterone is given during delivery and continued for a month or so afterwards, depression may be avoided.

If the problem is too high levels of prolactin after breast-feeding has ceased, the doctor may prescribe bromocriptine.

If you are taking either the combined oestrogen/progestogen contraceptive pill or the progestogen-only mini-pill, the doctor may well advise you to use another method of contraception. Not only is progestogen thought to lower the natural level of progesterone in the blood but the pill can encourage the menstrual clock to mark time, postponing the production of natural progesterone in the body.

A depression may even be a side-effect of the pill rather than true postnatal depression. If you have been on the pill, you may be advised to stop taking it or try a different brand, and to take pyridoxine or vitamin B6, which also helps some women suffering from pre-menstrual tension.

While your doctor may be able to give you or refer you for very specific help for postnatal depression, hormone treatment alone will not solve all your problems. It may help lift your mood enough so that the future stops looking totally hopeless but you also need to look for other ways to lighten your burden.

What commonly adds to the depression of a woman who has recently had a baby is that she tries to cope alone. She feels she is making a mess of motherhood, is a failure. All the other new mothers she knows seem to be pushing their prams proudly, enjoying their new role. If she did but know, half of them probably have doubts and low moments, if they're not downright depressed, and would be only too glad to exchange confidences. Talk about your feelings and worries and you will probably find many other mothers feel the same, and will certainly be sympathetic. No reasonable person will condemn you.

Don't be nervous about confiding in the health visitor, too. She will have come across many cases of postnatal depression before. She can be an invaluable source of sympathy and practical help, and may put you in touch with other mothers who would like to make friends.

It is particularly important to talk to friends if you are a single parent. If all the other new mothers you know have a partner and find it hard to appreciate the particular strains you have to cope with, do look for a local single parents group.

If you are married, remember the father is a parent just as much as you. Accept his offers of help, and when you are tired or feel low and edgy, ask him to look after the baby – and go away and do something else! Rest or have fun but don't hang around fretting and criticizing the way your husband does things.

Some mothers feel that only they know how to look after their child, criticize the way their husband handles the baby, feeds it, and so on, and eventually put him off becoming closely involved. As long as the baby is fed the right food, kept safe and has its nappy changed reasonably regularly, it will come to no harm. Just keep reminding yourself that you still have the right to some personal freedom, and set about arranging it.

Even if at first you don't feel up to talking to strangers, join a mothers' group in your area. This can be an absolute lifeline for many mothers. Ask neighbours for help – especially those who also have babies. Offer to look after their baby for a couple of hours in return for them looking after yours. Getting out for a break without the baby can be immensely refreshing. One mother I know put a card in her local newsagents saying she would like to meet others in a similar position. She formed friendships which lasted years and certainly tided her over the years at home with small children. I have listed organizations specifically for mothers in Reaching Out – see page 120 onwards.

Sexual problems after childbirth

Mothers suffering from even quite mild postnatal depression often have little or no interest in sex. Many couples date problems in their marriage and sex-life from having a baby. Of course, if the marriage was already under strain, a baby can add to the problems – indeed the pregnancy may have been a far from welcome surprise for one or both of them.

More general conflicts need to be explored in the ways we have already looked at in this book, but sexual problems after childbirth seem to contribute to the depression and anxiety of so many young mothers, so they need special explanation.

In fact, there are many quite natural reasons for not feeling like sex for some time after even a normal, fairly easy birth.

At the time of birth there are sudden, massive changes in the levels of the mother's hormones. Her body has to adapt and this takes time – particularly in the case of the hormones prolactin, oestrogen, progesterone and testosterone, all of which are involved in creating sexual desire.

Childbirth also causes massive physical changes in the womb and vagina, and it can take time for the tissues involved in the pleasurable feelings of intercourse and orgasm to regain sensitivity. If childbirth has caused a tear in the entrance to the vagina or, as is common, an episiotomy has been performed (a cut to widen the entrance), then this will have been stitched and may be very tender for some time. While the vagina is extremely elastic and returns to its normal size rapidly after a birth, you may find that the muscles at the entrance to the vagina are slacker, reducing sensation during intercourse for both you and your husband. For exercises to improve the tone of these muscles – see page 82.

Finally, like most women with a new baby you may be simply dog-tired – not the sort of comfortable sleepiness that can add to sensual pleasure but the drained exhaustion that causes you to crash out into oblivion the moment your head hits a pillow. This is very hard on your husband. He may have been thrilled to become a father but still feel very threatened by this third person whom he may subconsciously feel is a rival for your affections. He may resent the time you now spend fussing over the baby rather than him.

Many men feel inhibited from showing affection any way but sexually, so he may be all the more anxious to re-establish this side of your relationship, the part he feels just he and you share, which is apart from the baby. This can make him eager for intercourse before you feel ready for it. Even if you have fully recovered from the birth and any stitches, fear that it will hurt may make you involuntarily tense the muscles at the entrance to the vagina, making intercourse painful or impossible. The next time you try, the fear that it may be as bad again can be enough to ensure that it will be.

Even without experiencing actual pain, simply feeling pressured into intercourse you don't desire is enough to make the act – and your husband's touch – seem distasteful. If he persists, again it is a bad memory laid down to haunt the next time. Probably without realizing it, you may start finding ways to avoid sex.

ACTION PLAN

Share your feelings
If you're feeling anxious, exhausted, shut-out, say so. Give your partner the chance to reassure and comfort you. Try to explore any underlying conflicts.

Particularly if this is your first baby, you will both be feeling the strain of your new roles. You may be at home all day – at least for a few months – for the first time after working all your adult life. Even mothers who do not suffer from postnatal depression are commonly pretty wobbly and tearful at this stage. No matter how high-powered a job you had before, sole responsibility for a tiny baby is a very different matter and it can seem nerve-wracking.

Your partner may be feeling pretty frightened himself in his new role as a father, and worried about financial responsibilities if he is going to be sole breadwinner for a while.

Share your feelings about sex, too. If you don't feel like

intercourse, say so but make it clear that it's the intercourse you're temporarily refusing, not the man.

Keep in touch
Make an effort to stay physically close. The trap many couples fall into is that, because the wife – or perhaps the husband – doesn't feel like intercourse, they barely touch one another.

If you keep kissing, cuddling and caressing, it helps in two ways. You can both feel reassured that you are still loved and desired, and it helps your hormones resume their natural function in the build-up of desire. Sexual appetite tends to increase the more it is fed.

When you feel you cannot even bear your husband's touch, it may be because you interpret it as an unspoken demand for intercourse. If you can enjoy the caresses without feeling that you *must* go on to intercourse, after a time you'll probably find that you want to, of your own accord. In the meantime, you can still bring one another to climax, if you want to, without having intercourse.

Put yourselves first at least sometimes
What often happens after having a baby is that you spend all your time and energy on looking after the baby, keeping the house presentable for visitors, cooking, washing. Superwo-mum! Settle for looking after the baby and your relationship. Keep time for you and your husband to relax together.

Give yourselves time
Don't panic if you still don't feel like sex after a month or two but do be sensible about when you are going to try. Just because you always used to go to bed at 11 p.m. and make love, it's unrealistic to expect to go on doing so if you have a baby who wakes for his feed at 11.15 p.m.

Most mothers find that their baby's cry switches on an internal alarm system that switches off all other feelings. No matter how resentful it makes your husband, you won't be able to go on making love while the baby cries in the next room.

The time to start snuggling up is the second the baby has nodded off after a feed, whether it's seven in the morning or two o'clock during a weekend afternoon. You may well find that seizing the moment actually adds to your satisfaction. And if you don't feel like suggesting sex, then offer – or ask for – a massage. Loving attention can carry you safely through many weeks without intercourse.

TEN

No Longer A Woman?

The menopause has a terrible image. Menopausal women are supposed to be tearful, irrational, suffer from hot flushes and even be likely to go shop-lifting. In fact, research shows that women in this age group on the whole suffer less from symptoms such as absent-mindedness, irritability and depression, than do younger women.

You may think that is cold comfort if you *are* depressed, anxious and miserable. But it will help you to tackle your depression if you sort out which of your problems can be laid at the door of the change of life, and which are to do with other pressures in your life which happen to coincide with the menopause.

Mid-life can be a time of many changes and pressures. Children may leave home and some couples discover that they then have very little left to say to one another. Parents may die or there may be worries over the future of elderly and infirm parents, stirring up feelings left over from child-hood. It is a time, too, for realizing that dreams as yet unfulfilled are likely to stay that way – which can create a sense of hopelessness. And while there is no physical reason why most couples should not continue to enjoy an active sex life, the sexual slowing down many men experience at this time and disturbances caused by the menopause can combine with sexual difficulties and disappointments built up over the years, so that a couple lose this warm link between them.

If you are depressed and also going through the menopause, please don't assume that you will find all the answers you need in this chapter alone – the earlier chapters are also relevant and helpful. Read, and try to follow up, the suggestions made there.

You may find others – including your husband – show resistance to the idea that your depression and anxiety can't simply be blamed on to your 'time of life' and that they need to become involved if you are to resolve your problems. See your doctor, by all means, to check whether you need specific treatment, but make it clear to everyone involved that your menopause isn't going to carry the can for problems such as your husband showing you no affection, or you being expected to cope single-handed with a job, running the home, and a sick parent five miles away.

Even if your depression is in part due to the menopause, it is simply one piece in the jigsaw and you will need to explore your feelings deeply.

Most women rather welcome the idea that they can no longer get pregnant, need no longer worry about taking contraceptive precautions, but some have mixed emotions about the end of the possibility of child-bearing. If, for one reason or another, you never had the family you wanted, you may react to the definite end of your hopes of ever having children with a deep depression. You may feel that your femininity is very much tied up with the ability to have children and that when your periods have ceased it is impossible for you still to be an attractive woman. These feelings of loss cannot simply be dismissed. If they bother you, do talk about them, in the ways suggested on page 28. If you give expression to the grief you feel, you will better be able to take a positive approach to the menopause.

Certainly there is no need these days to believe that it spells the end of anything, except the ability to bear a child. The only symptom of the menopause experienced by all women is the stopping of monthly periods.

During a woman's child-bearing years the ovaries release an egg approximately once a month. They also produce the hormones oestrogen and progesterone which cause the womb to prepare a thick lining in case the egg is fertilized. If the egg is not fertilized, the uterus sheds its lining with the extra blood intended to feed the egg. This passes out through the vagina as a period.

At the menopause, which can occur any time between the ages of thirty-nine to fifty-six, and in certain cases even earlier or later, the ovaries slow down production of oestrogen and progesterone. This may happen in a smooth, even decline, with periods getting lighter and lighter and eventually ceasing altogether. It may happen suddenly –

without warning, you simply have no more periods. Usually, however, it happens in fits and starts, with periods varying in their spacing, heaviness and duration as the hormone levels fluctuate.

Progesterone is thought to promote a sense of calm and contentment, so a sudden lack of it might lead a woman to feel the reverse, upsetting her emotional balance and aggravating sleeping problems. It also leads to a drying and thinning of the vaginal walls, and lubrication during intercourse may be slower. It is thought to affect bone formation and is connected with osteoporosis, a condition that causes brittle bones in old age.

It also seems likely that hot flushes – the most common symptom of the menopause, apart from the stopping of periods – are caused by low oestrogen levels. Changes in the levels of oestrogen probably affect the body's heat regulating system which sends blood to the surface of the skin to cool us off. Blushing in puberty coincides with the reproductive system revving up, hot flushes in the menopause coincide with its slowing down.

If you are already feeling anxious and depressed, and find it a great strain to go out and meet people, then being subject to hot flushes can seem like the final straw. You may feel silly and embarrassed, and in the end too distressed to go anywhere – which adds to your depression. It's another vicious circle.

While hot flushes can't be said only to have psychological causes, certainly, the more you worry that in a particular situation you will have a hot flush, the more likely you are to have one. Also, the more embarrassed you feel once it starts, the worse it is likely to get.

If you check in a mirror you will probably find that what feels like a fiery crimson looks like only a rosy glow, if it is noticeable at all. Remind yourself, too, that you would never dislike someone or disapprove of them because they had a hot flush, so why on earth should anyone hold it against you. Taking several deep breaths and consciously relaxing your muscles, as explained on page 12, helps. If you can slip away and hold your wrists, with the hands palm upwards, under the cold tap, it may help. Hot drinks and alcohol can trigger a hot flush so avoid these at times you particularly want to avoid flushing.

Lack of oestrogen can be connected with loss of calcium from the bones, causing them to be more vulnerable to breaks in the event of a fall. However, this can be treated with hormone replacement therapy – of which more in a minute. You can also effectively prevent or lessen this effect with exercise, which is a very important bone strengthener, as well as keeping joints supple, muscles toned, and helping prevent gynaecological problems.

At the menopause many women find that their body needs less fuel, so if they carry on eating and exercising the same amount as before they tend to put on weight. A sensible diet – not a punishing one – and regular exercise will preserve your figure and safeguard your health, particularly by guarding against heart disease. Do check with your doctor before taking up new types of exercise, but following the suggestions on pages 63–72 will minimize the effects of the menopause. It is perfectly possible to stay slim, fit and active into your seventies and eighties.

Some women find the drying and thinning of the vaginal walls *increases* sexual pleasure – the firmer vagina giving increased sensation. Others find that it causes pain and itching. Because sex is uncomfortable it becomes less frequent and because it is less frequent, the vagina becomes less able to respond. Patience can be one answer – more time for love-play can encourage more lubrication.

Replacement lubrication for the vagina, such as KY Jelly, which is safe, colourless and odourless, can make sex a great deal more comfortable. Or your doctor may prescribe hormone cream for local application.

Hormone replacement therapy (HRT) in tablet form may help — (see page 105) – but hormones are not aphrodisiacs. They can help to make sex more comfortable – though HRT is unlikely to be prescribed for this purpose alone – but hormones cannot create an interest in sex which isn't already there, particularly if it has been absent for years.

Some women find that the altered hormone balance at the menopause leads to an increased sex drive while others – particularly those also suffering from depression at this time – complain that they have lost interest in sex.

You have to try to disentangle the myth and its effects

from the reality. There is no reason for any woman to feel that the menopause spells the end of her enjoyable sex life.

Women who have taken the attitude that 'Of course, all that sort of thing ends with the change of life', probably wanted it that way. That's fair enough, it's their choice though it may be sad that they and their partner didn't discover how to make sex a more mutually satisfying experience that they would want to continue.

Unfortunately, the myth put about by women who actually wanted to stop sexual activity can discourage others who enjoy sex and want to carry on doing so but run into a crisis of confidence at this time. Hormonal changes at the menopause do *not* cause you physically to lose your ability to enjoy sex. Your depression may coincide with the menopause, but it is almost certainly the depression which is causing any lowered sex drive, and it will respond to treatment with the self-help exercises on page 80 onwards – aided by added lubrication or HRT, if that has been prescribed for you.

Hormone replacement therapy

The ovaries don't stop functioning completely after the menopause but other parts of the body, such as the adrenal gland and fatty tissue under the skin, become the main sources of oestrogen and progesterone. Some women produce enough to prevent symptoms caused by lack of oestrogen – thought to be the main culprit in menopausal problems with a hormonal base. Others, troubled by severe hot flushes and night sweats, vaginal problems, or marked osteoporosis, may benefit from hormone replacement therapy. HRT will not solve all your troubles and keep you forever youthful and sexy – there's no escaping the hard work you must put in yourself to achieve that sort of goal. However, if you are suffering very severe physical symptoms which are making it harder than ever for you to tackle other problems, then hormone replacement therapy may help.

Doctors vary in their attitude to HRT. A few are very much in favour of it and believe in prescribing it for virtually the rest of a woman's life. They point out that a woman's natural life span used to mean that she lived only a few years beyond the menopause whereas now she will probably live for a further quarter of a century. They say the *unnatural* thing is to expect her to live without hormone supplements. More commonly, other doctors believe that the cause of problems is a *sudden* decline in oestrogen or an individual woman's body having difficulty in adapting to the change, so HRT is likely to be needed for perhaps a couple of years to smooth the transition. Some doctors are reluctant to try HRT at all, believing that there are serious risks associated with tampering with hormone levels.

Oestrogen used *alone* to treat the symptoms of the menopause was found to be linked with an increased risk of cancer of the womb, so it is usually given with progestogen supplements which guard against this. Your doctor may advize against oestrogen treatment if you have high blood pressure, smoke heavily, are overweight, or suffer from problems such as diabetes.

Whether you will be helped by hormone replacement therapy is something to discuss in detail with your doctor. He may give you a very sensible explanation why it is not right for you but I would not be satisfied by a doctor who simply rejected the suggestion that it might help without discussion, or brushed my anxieties and unhappiness aside. If your doctor is very dismissive about 'women's problems' (I'm afraid that a few still exist), do consider changing doctors. There is little point in having a doctor you can't talk to comfortably.

Hysterectomy and mastectomy

Hysterectomy is the second commonest operation performed on women; by the age of seventy-five one in five will have had her womb removed. However, it is increasingly being questioned whether the operation is necessary as often as it is performed. Women who have hysterectomies are four times as likely to become depressed within three years of the operation. Nearly three-quarters of women who have hysterectomies suffer from depression afterwards.

Mastectomy – removal of a breast, usually because of cancer – is not so common but it is very often followed by depression. It may have been life-saving, but the woman has not only lost a part of her female identity but the loss is one clearly visible to herself and to her sexual partner.

If you have had, or are about to have, an operation of this kind, it is important that you and those close to you realize that you should expect to feel very unhappy over it, to grieve. It is absolutely natural to feel sorrow in such circumstances but the doctors and nurses you see may dismiss your feelings, partly because they may have had no training in coping with distress in others, in helpful ways to offer sympathy, and partly because they may see the operation in purely medical terms, as something to improve or safeguard your health. They may not want to face up to the other implications.

Your family may be so relieved to know that the operation will help you that they may not be prepared for your sorrow. Others may be embarrassed to talk about what is actually being done, not like to think about the facts of the operation itself.

But if you suppress your grief, you are more likely to suffer from severe depression later, so do find someone you can confide in and see Reaching Out – pages 120–124 – for information about special groups. If you know someone who has had a similar operation you can bring one another great comfort by sharing your feelings. If you don't know anyone personally, ask your doctor if he could suggest another patient who might talk to you. He can always contact her first to check that she is willing.

If your doctor tells you that you need a mastectomy, do ask him to explain exactly why he feels the operation is necessary. Sometimes, for example, removal of the whole breast is not necessary in order to stop cancer spreading. If your doctor believes that it is essential then in the end you have to rely on his judgement. But make it clear that this is very important to you and you need to be sure that such major surgery is essential.

There is no doubt that some hysterectomies are performed unnecessarily and that, sometimes, healthy ovaries are removed along with a diseased womb. If you are told that you should have a hysterectomy, ask whether this is really the only treatment available and what will be the consequences if you don't have your womb removed. Sometimes, of course, it is essential and will save your life, but there may be alternatives. If you must have your womb removed ask if it is necessary to have your ovaries removed also. Some surgeons take the view that 'you're not going to need these any more' and remove healthy, functioning ovaries along with the womb. This can have serious consequences if you have not yet completed the menopause because it suddenly deprives your body of the ovaries' hormone supplies and you may suffer severe menopausal symptoms. If the doctor is not sure whether your ovaries are healthy, make it clear to him – and in writing on the consent form – that they are only to be removed if there is evidence of disease.

For many women the cervix, the neck of the womb protruding into the vagina, plays an important role in sexual responsiveness, so if this is removed along with the womb, sexual enjoyment may be impaired. Ask your doctor if the cervix can be left in place even if the womb must be removed. To lose your enjoyment of sex after the operation would obviously increase the likelihood of depression.

If you find it difficult to ask your doctor for more information about what is being done to your body and why, read again the suggestions about learning to be more assertive – see page 44. He may have the medical training but it is *your* body and you have to live with the consequences of the operation, not him.

ELEVEN

Home and Away

If you are reading this book because someone close to you – your wife, mother, friend – is suffering from depression, you probably need some sympathy yourself. Living with someone who's depressed can be very gruelling. You sit and listen to their woes one day, spend a lot of time and energy comforting them, and the next day you go through the whole process all over again.

However, it is absolutely crucial that anyone who is depressed feels able to share her innermost thoughts and feelings openly, knowing that she can rely on you not to throw them back in her face at a later stage.

Give her plenty of time to talk without interruption. You will be of more help than you may realize if you can just sit quietly and say 'Mmmm' encouragingly at appropriate moments. Put an arm round her, or rest your hand on her arm – establish contact in some way. Touch can be far more reassuring than words, but in our culture we tend to lose the habit. Resist the temptation to interrupt with similar experiences of your own. We tend to say, 'Oh, I felt down just like you when ...' That takes attention away from her feelings and, since she's the one suffering from depression at the moment, it is her feelings that need the release.

Don't expect any suggestions you make to be followed up. Meaning well, we often say, 'What you need to do is get out more, join a club, give him a piece of your mind ...' Chances are she is not at that stage yet, and all you will achieve is to make her feel you don't really understand just how depressed she is. Remember that what works for one person may not help another. Offer any ideas that may help, but don't be hurt and angry if they are rejected. This just adds to the feelings of guilt and loneliness of the depressed.

Look after yourself, too. Depression can be contagious. Make sure you spend some time every day with other friends or members of your family. This will help stop you getting sucked in and seeing the world in the same gloomy way. Give yourself a few treats, too, to remind yourself that there is a brighter side to life. This will also better enable you to help the one who is depressed, since it will build up your resilience and strength.

Just about everything in the sections on relaxation, exercise and healthy eating applies as much to you as it does to anyone suffering from depression. All of us undergo stress, all of us need to safeguard ourselves against ill-effects. Keep a check on what stress symptoms *you* are showing. Remember that many people, particularly men, try to 'contain' stress for years and then suffer physical ill-effects. If your partner is depressed, it could be an early-warning sign for both of you. Certainly you can best help someone who is anxious and/or depressed to start taking action to relieve stress and tension if you join in rather than stand on the sidelines saying, '*You* should do this and that.'

Try to join in with any plan to start exercising or eating more healthily; be interested and encouraging. Don't cover up your own lack of enthusiasm and incentive by jeering. Don't resist her efforts to set aside a little time regularly to care for herself. Remember, a partner or friend who is depressed has a lot to gain by starting to look after herself – so have you.

Particularly if you are the husband of a woman suffering from depression, you may have read with mixed feelings some of what I've said about women needing to learn to be assertive, to put their own needs first sometimes. I am not painting you as the villain of the piece. In fact, if you take the trouble to read this book you are obviously very sympathetic and want to do all you can to help your wife recover.

I have to generalize and there undoubtedly is a tendency for women to suppress their drive and swallow anger. This is not your fault. All I am suggesting is that women should take more responsibility for their own lives and happiness. You may find it a relief to live with someone who regards herself as your equal. Even if it demands a few adjustments on your part, it is going to be preferable to living with someone suffering from depression.

Obviously it will help if *you* are flexible and prepared to change. If your partner starts to tell you how something you do upsets her, resist the temptation simply to say 'Oh, but that doesn't mean I don't love you.' She will feel you are dismissing what she is trying to tell you. Whatever you mean, it *does* make her feel unloved or frustrated. Listen to what she is saying, accept her feelings. She will do the same for you.

If it's a friend who is depressed, then encourage her to make a list of what can and can't be changed, if she can't at first summon up the energy. You will probably find it quite illuminating applied to your own life, too. And you can compare lists.

There is, of course, a limit to what can be achieved by self-help, particularly in cases of serious depression. Do consider whether your partner or friend should consult her doctor if she hasn't done so already. Her depression may be so severe that she needs medical help.

However, I hope too, that all I have said about the doctor not providing a magic cure has made sense to you. If the doctor believes that anti-depressants will help – then you may see a marked improvement after a couple of weeks. You may need to help the sufferer through those weeks by putting up with side-effects without experiencing benefits. But, particularly if it is your partner who is depressed, also be prepared for some uncomfortable heart-searching. She is ill, and at least part of the cause probably lies in your relationship, even if it is simply that you do not confide in one another. It can make a tremendous difference if you are prepared to accept your involvement in both the problem and the treatment.

When should you seek outside help?

If you are seriously depressed for two weeks or more, and feel you are stuck in the depression or getting worse, do consult your doctor. People sometimes do not realize that they are suffering from depression, they cannot imagine that the world need not seem as black as it does to them. Mothers with young children who are suffering from quite serious depression often do not seek help – probably partly because of the difficulties of getting to see their doctor when they have young children, but partly because they almost take it for granted that they should feel so bad.

If it is your partner, a member of your family or a friend who has been very depressed for more than a couple of weeks and has not sought her doctor's help, then do suggest this course of action. If she seems too listless even to arrange it, offer to make the appointment and escort her there.

Depression can be a fatal illness. You should not hesitate to get medical help yourself, directly, if you think that the depressed person may be suicidal. How can you tell?

- Don't believe the old wives' tale that those who talk about killing themselves don't do it. Four out of five people who commit suicide have talked about it. Talking about suicide or loneliness is a danger signal.

- Watch out for signs that she is preparing for death. Some people clear out their drawers, make a will, sort out their personal belongings, talk about life insurance policies or give away a prized possession. Combined with depression, these are all danger signals.

- Any indication that she is stockpiling medicines is a very definite warning. Even if you are confident that there is no risk of attempted suicide, do make sure that anyone seriously depressed has a careful routine for taking her drugs that safeguards against accidents, and that drugs are not kept by the bed. Tactfully make sure that she is following her doctor's instructions, and not mixing prescription drugs with over-the-counter drugs he knows nothing about.

- Don't think that because she has talked about suicide before and not tried, or made what you might call a very 'half-hearted' attempt, that she will not try again and perhaps succeed. She may be trying to manipulate you, to gain more sympathy, but such despair deserves sympathy. Don't be tempted to dare her to carry out her threats. You'll be alive if you are wrong, but she won't, and you'll never forgive yourself.

- Don't fall into the trap of thinking that the very religious will be protected by their beliefs from attempting suicide.

They both try and succeed.

If you notice any of these danger signals, get medical advice without delay. The Samaritans can be very helpful. If you think there is any risk of the depressed person trying to commit suicide, don't leave her alone, not even to go to the lavatory. Get someone else to ask for help.

When home is not the best place

These days most people suffering from depression can be treated at home by their GP. However, in cases of severe depression, a hospital is sometimes the best place to maintain 24-hours-a-day vigilance. It is unlikely that a doctor will advise admission to hospital unless he believes it is essential.

Some people are still very apprehensive of psychiatric hospitals, thinking of them as the funny farm or loony bin where people are locked away, but these days the vast majority of patients are admitted voluntarily and spend only a few weeks or months in hospital.

More psychiatric hospital beds are occupied by people suffering from depression than from any other condition and to go into psychiatric hospital is now a common experience – one in twelve of all men and one in eight women is admitted at least once during their lifetime.

If you are severely depressed you may actually greet the suggestion that you should go into hospital with relief, since it means that your illness is being taken seriously. If you know you are very ill, and are worrying what effect you are having on the family, you may welcome the idea of leaving home for a while. Sometimes the family may be part of the cause of the depression and a break from the home may itself help start the cure.

Obviously some psychiatric hospitals are spoken of more highly than others, and some psychiatric disturbances are easier to treat than others. Patients who have been treated for depression in hospital seem generally afterwards to appreciate the help they have received and some talk with great feeling about the caring treatment of the staff.

Pamela agreed to go into a local psychiatric hospital reluctantly.

I didn't want to go into hospital, with the family to look after, but the psychiatrist said it was that or my health. One more crisis and I'd go over the top.

The trouble really started while I was waiting for a hysterectomy operation. First, I had a terrible row with my mother. I'd asked if she was coming to stay for Christmas, and she said no. Then my father phoned to ask if he could come – they'd separated when I was small. I said, 'Of course.' A couple of days afterwards my mother said could she come after all.

During the row over that the phone rang – it was a hospital in London saying my father had collapsed. He died before I could get there.

My parents split up when I was five. I remember sitting on my father's knee and being asked who did I want to go with, mummy or daddy? A terrible experience. It was my last memory of him until I was much older.

I was evacuated after that. My mother didn't want to be with her kids at all, she had them and that was it, she just wanted to dump them. She started living with another man. I did come home again, but she didn't like housework and we had to do it all. She did go out to work, but you don't expect a seven-year-old to scrub floors, do you? I did the darning, the ironing, the shopping. When she hit us, she didn't just hit – she used to jump on us. Once she threw a carving knife at my brother and it stuck in the wall, having missed his ear by a hair's breadth.

I got back in touch with my Dad in my teens. He was thrilled to see me. It was my father who introduced me to my husband, who was working with him – I was eighteen when I got married.

When I heard my father had died without my even seeing him I was in the pit of despair. Then I went into hospital and had the hysterectomy. My mother didn't come to see me or even send a card, though I got an infection because I'm allergic to penicillin which nearly killed me.

Afterwards I just went down and down. I felt as if nobody cared, nobody knew what I was going through. Why, I don't know. I had everything to live for – four children, a lovely home. It's stupid, really – the more people say 'snap out of it, pull yourself together', the more you think they don't understand. I got into such a state that I phoned the doctor and told him that if I had a gas oven I'd put my head in it. So he came round, gave me some tranquillizers and fixed me an appointment with a psychiatrist.

The psychiatrist saw me straight away. I told him I couldn't understand why I felt so bad and he said 'Your mind has had so much all at once. It all stems from your childhood, having such a rough time. The row with your mother, your father dying – it's too much.'

He said I should go into hospital and I was in for nine weeks. They gave me some tablets (major tranquillizers) three times a day, which knocked me out. Gradually, I began to feel better. The tablets helped and the psychiatrist was a very understanding man. He wasn't one of these who stopped you, he let you talk it out. This is one of the things I had missed.

I couldn't talk to my husband, He knew how depressed I was but couldn't understand why. When my father died, I wanted to talk about it, but my husband kept saying, 'Don't talk about it.' He meant it in the nicest possible way – he thought talking about it would make me *more* depressed. It didn't. It relieved the tension.

I started panicking when the doctor said he was going to send me home. He gave me a supply of tablets but said to try and gradually work myself off them. I did, and kept on going back to see him, until he said at last that I'd got over it nicely. Touch wood, I have.

It was a crisis and I did get over it, but saying snap out of it is the worst thing that anyone can say. However much you want to, and however much you try, you just can't. You really do need help. You need someone to notice.

For many women, like Pamela, hospital provides the safe, ordered environment, free of responsibilities, which they need to weather a serious crisis, but patients and their relatives sometimes have anxieties about the treatment prescribed. A patient may particularly dislike the side-effects of a drug, for example, or be worried about the risks of electro-convulsive therapy. A voluntary patient cannot be forced to undergo any treatment against her will, though if she persistently refuses the treatment recommended the doctors may in the end say that she must leave the hospital since there is nothing more they can do to help her.

Don't feel you must accept all the treatment suggested however, if you have serious reservations about it. If in your heart of hearts you believe it may damage you, then the risk that you will suffer unfortunate side-effects are considerably increased. Ask the doctors to explain exactly what is involved, what is known about the safety and risks of treatment, how they believe it will help, what alternatives are available.

If it is your partner who is being advised treatment, remember that people suffering from depression are by the very nature of their illness often negative. When you discuss treatments with them they may belittle any improvements, see only the disadvantages and not the benefits. Before reaching your own conclusions, do discuss the treatments and its side-effects with the doctor.

Patients who are admitted to psychiatric hospital against their will, because they are thought to be a danger to themselves or others may in some circumstances be given treatment against their wishes – if it is thought that without treatment they may attempt suicide, or make a further attempt. If you want to object to treatment the legal position is not clear cut and you should seek advice on your particular case – see Reaching Out, pages 118 and 124.

Usually a spell in hospital will bring about a dramatic improvement in someone suffering from severe depression, in which event it can be tempting to draw a veil over the whole illness and what led up to it. Of course, no-one wants to dwell on unhappy memories – and it could tend to encourage the depression to return – but even after hospital treatment it is important to bear in mind the causes of depression and the self-help ways to guard against it discussed in this book.

TWELVE

Reaching Out

It may be the day you first laugh again, or give someone you love a spontaneous hug. You may realize you are looking forward to a family outing at the weekend or have simply thoroughly enjoyed the meal you've just eaten, or a good night's sleep. All kinds of little signs, that might not sound much to anyone who has not known the grey and lustreless landscape of depression, can let you know that you are on the road up and out.

Don't be tempted to rest on your laurels at that point. It is easy to think, 'Oh, that's all right then. I'm getting better. I needn't make any more special efforts, life can go back to how it was before.' It was almost certainly 'life as it was before' that led to your depression, or was at least part of the problem, and it could do again.

Try not to relinquish new-found habits of sharing your feelings, caring for your own needs as well as those of others, looking after your body and keeping it well-exercised and healthy. If you look around you, you will find there are plenty of other women who have known the same difficulties as you, and who are finding different ways to tackle them. Do seek out their support, and that of the special organizations trying to help women with a whole variety of problems which can lead to depression. It is feeling alone with your worries that can so often turn a difficult time into a depressing one but, in fact, no matter how troubled you are, you never need feel alone again. Here are some of the places you can turn to for help.

Learning to relax

Relaxation for Living, 29 Burwood Park Road, Walton-on-Thames, Surrey KT12 5LH (093–22 27826) provides information, cassette tapes, etc. and runs groups in many parts of the country.

Stresswatch, P.O. Box 4AR, London W1A 4AR helps people with anxiety and phobic difficulties.

Stress Syndrome Foundation, Cedar House, Yalding, Kent ME18 6JD (0622 814431) supplies information about stress-related problems. Send for publications list.

Phobics Society, 4 Cheltenham Road, Manchester M21 IQ2 (061–881 1937) advises on any type of phobia.

Open Door Association, 447 Pensby Road, Heswall, Wirral L61 9PQ (051–648 2022) helps sufferers from agoraphobia.

Lifestyle Training Centre, 23 Abingdon Road, London W8 (01–938 1011) supplies books and cassette tapes on relaxation, and coping with anxiety, depression and phobias.

Wheel of Yoga, 80 Leckhampton Road, Cheltenham, Glos. GL53 0BN.

Siddha Yoga Dham, 15 Fitzroy Square, London W1P 5HQ (01–387 4185) teaches a natural process of meditation.

Teach-yourself books

The Massage Book by George Downing, Penguin.

The Art of Sensual Massage by Gordon Inkeles and Murray Todris, Allen and Unwin.

Self-help for your Nerves, Peace from Nervous Suffering, Agoraphobia by Dr Claire Weekes, Angus & Robertson, and cassette tapes available through Mrs Joyce Skene-Keating, 16 Rivermead Court, Ranelagh Gardens, London SW6 3RT.

Auto-hypnosis by Ronald Shore, Thorsons.

Talking it through

MIND (National Association for Mental Health), 22 Harley Street, London, W1N 2ED (01–637 0741) has comprehensive information about services available.

Samaritans: local numbers listed in telephone directory and in possession of operator. Head Office: 17 Uxbridge Road, Slough SL1 1SN (0753 32713).

Cruse, Cruse House, 126 Sheen Road, Richmond, Surrey TW9 1UR (01–940 4818) offers bereavement counselling for the widowed.

Depressives Anonymous, 83 Derby Road, Nottingham NG1 5BB, for information about self-help groups.

National Marriage Guidance Council, Little Church Street, Rugby, Warwicks. CV21 3AP (0788 73241).

Scottish Marriage Guidance Council, 58 Palmerston Place, Edinburgh EH12 5AZ (031–225 5006).

Catholic Marriage Advisory Council, 15 Lansdowne Road, London W11 3AJ (01–727 0141).

Jewish Marriage Council, 529b Finchley Road, London NW3 6LS (01–794 5222).

British Association for Counselling, 37a Sheep Street, Rugby CV21 3BX (0788 78328).

National Youth Bureau, 17–23 Albion Street, Leicester LE1 6GD (0533 554775) for under-25s.

Association for Marriage Enrichment, c/o Westminster Pastoral Foundation, 23 Kensington Square, London W8 5HN (01–937 6956) teaches techniques to improve communication between couples.

Association for Humanistic Psychology, 62 Southwark Bridge Road, London SE1 0AS (01–928 8254) can provide information of groups and courses to help people improve their personal relationships.

British Association of Psychotherapists, 121 Hendon Lane, London N3 (01–346 1747).

National Council of Psychotherapists Hypnotherapy Register, 1 Clovelly Road, London W5 5HS (01–567 0262).

Psychotherapy Centre and British Hypnotherapy Association, 67 Upper Berkeley Street, London W1H 7DH (01–723 6173).

Women's Therapy Centre, 19a Hartman Road, London N7 provides group and individual psychotherapy for women only.

A Woman In Your Own Right: Assertiveness and You by Anne Dickson, Quartet.

The Courage to Grieve by Judy Tatelbaum, Heinemann.

Health and Fitness

Health Education Council, 78 New Oxford Street, London WC1 1AH (01–637 1881) for general advice and information.

Scottish Health Education Unit, 21 Lansdowne Crescent, Edinburgh EH12 5EH (031 447 8044).

Physical Fitness contains the Canadian Air Force exercises, Penguin.

The Health and Fitness Handbook edited by Miriam Polunin, Sphere.

Sports Council (England), 16 Upper Woburn Place, WC1H 0QP (01–388 1277 Ext. 224) for further information about sports and facilities.

Sports Council (Wales), National Sports Centre for Wales, Sophia Garden, Cardiff CF1 9SW (0222 397571).

Sports Council (Scotland), 1 St Colme Street, Edinburgh EH3 6AA (031–2258411).

Sports Council (Northern Ireland), House of Sport, 2a Upper Malone Road, Belfast BT9 (0232 661222).

Keep Fit Association, 16 Upper Woburn Place, WC1H 0QP (01–387 4349) for women only.

Ramblers Association, 1–5 Wandsworth Road, London SW8 2LJ (01–582 6878).

Family Planning Information Service, 27–35 Mortimer Street, London W1N 7RJ (01–636 7866) for information on contraception and most aspects of women's health.

Women's Health Concern, 16 Seymour Street, London W1H 5WB (01–486 8653) provides information on problems such as PMT and the menopause.

Well Woman Centre, Marie Stopes House, 108 Whitfield Street, London W1P 6BE (01–388 0662/2585).

New interests, new friends

National Association of Women's Clubs, 5 Vernon Rise, Kings Cross Road, London WC1X 9EP (01–837 1434).

National Housewives Register, 245 Warwick Road, Solihull, West Midlands B91 7AH (021–706 1101) for the 'lively minded woman'.

National Federation of Women's Institutes, 39 Eccleston Street, Victoria, London SW1W 9NT (01–730 7212).

National Union of Townswomen's Guilds, Chamber of Commerce House, 75 Harborne Road, Edgbaston, Birmingham B15 3DA (021–455 6868).

Women's Royal Voluntary Service, 17 Old Park Lane, London W1Y 4AJ (01–499 6040).

National Federation of 18 plus groups of Great Britain, Nicholson House, Old Court Road, Newent, Gloucestershire (0531 821210) for 18–30 year olds.

National Youth Bureau, 17–23 Albion Street, Leicester LE1 6GD (0533 554775) for under-25s.

Volunteer Centre, 29 Lower Kings Road, Berkhamstead, Herts HP4 2AB (04427 73311).

National Council for Voluntary Organisations, 26 Bedford Square, London WC1B 3HU (01–636 4066).

National Institute of Adult Continuing Education, 19b de Montfort Street, Leicester LE1 7GE (0533 551451).

National Extension College, 18 Brooklands Avenue, Cambridge CB2 2HN (0223 63465).

Open University, P.O. Box 188, Milton Keynes MK3 6HW, runs many non-academic courses as well as those leading to degrees.

National Council for Civil Liberties, 21 Tabard Street, London SE1 4LA (01–403 3888) includes Women's Rights Unit.

Women's Information and Referral Service (WIRES), P.O. Box 162, Sheffield 1 1UD (0742 755290). Can supply details of women's consciousness-raising and mental health groups.

Women's Research and Resources Centre, Hungerford House, Victoria Embankment, London WC2 (01–930 0715).

Spare Rib, 27 Clerkenwell Close, London EC1R 0AT. The 'notice board' of the women's movement.

Meet-a-Mum Association (MAMA), 26a Cumnor Hill, Oxford OX2 9HA (0865 863258).

Pre-School Playgroups Association, Alford House, Aveline Street, London SE11 5DH (01–582 8871).

Gingerbread, 35 Wellington Street, London WC2 E7BN (01–240 0953) for lone parents.

National Federation of Solo Clubs, Room 8, Ruskin Chambers, 191 Corporation Street, Birmingham B4 6RY. (021–236 2879) for singles over 25, separated, divorced and widowed.

National Council for the Divorced and Separated, 13 High Street, Little Shelford, Cambridge CB2 5ES.

Scottish Single, Widowed, Divorced and Separated Clubs, 103 McCulloch Street, Glasgow G41.

Cruse, 126 Sheen Road, Richmond, Surrey TW9 1UR (01–940 4818/9047) for the widowed.

National Federation of Old Age Pension Associations, 91 Preston New Road, Blackburn, Lancs BB2 6BD (0254 52606).

Outsiders Club, P.O. Box 4ZB, London W1A 4ZB (01–741 3332) for those who feel some physical or social handicap makes it difficult for them to make friends and find someone to love.

Help with particular problems

Age Concern (England) 60 Pitcairn Road, Mitcham, Surrey CR4 3LL (01–640 5431).

Action on Alcohol Abuse, Dept. of Community Medicine, Usher Institute, Warrender Park Road, Edinburgh EH9 1DW (031–229 6207).

Alcoholics Anonymous, P.O. Box 514, 11 Redcliffe Gardens, London SW10 9BG (01–352 9779) for outside London, and 140a Tachbrook Street, London SW1V 2NE (for callers in London).

Al-Anon Family Groups, 61 Great Dover Street, London SE1 4YS (01–403 0888).

Drinkwatchers (01–727 9447) help develop sensible drinking habits.

Action Against Allergy, 43 The Downs, London SW20 8HG (01–947 5082).

Anorexic Aid, Priory Centre, 11 Priory Road, High Wycombe, Bucks HP13 63L.

Cancer Link, 12 Cressy Road, London NW3 2LY (01–267 8048).

Association for New Approaches to Cancer, 231 Kensal Road, London W10 5DB (01–969 1684).

National Association of Carers, c/o Medway Homes, Balfour Road, Rochester, Kent ME4 6QU (0634 813981).

National Council for Carers and their Elderly Dependants, 29 Chilworth Mews, London W2 3RG (01–262 1451/2).

National Association for the Childless, 318 Summer Lane, Birmingham B19 3RL (021–359 4887).

Compassionate Friends, 5 Lower Clifton Hill, Clifton, Bristol BS8 1BT (0272 292778) for bereaved parents.

Stillbirth and Neonatal Death Society (SANDS), 37 Christchurch Hill, London NW3 1LA (01–794 4601).

National Childbirth Trust, 9 Queensborough Terrace, London W2 3TB (01–221 3833).

When Pregnancy Fails: Coping with Miscarriage, Stillbirth and Infant Death by Susan Borg and Judith Lasker, Routledge & Kegan Paul.

Depression After Childbirth by Katharina Dalton, Oxford University Press.

Association for Postnatal Illness, 7 Gowan Avenue, London SW6.

National Council for the Divorced and Separated, 13 High Street, Little Shelford, Cambridge CB2 5ES.

Royal Association for Disability & Rehabilitation, 25 Mortimer Street, London W1N 8AB (01–637 5400).

Institute for Drug Dependence, 3 Blackburn Road, London NW6 1XA (01–328 5541).

Release, 1 Elgin Avenue, London W9 3TR (01–603 8654) for problems connected with drug dependence.

Fat Is A Feminist Issue by Susie Orbach, Hamlyn, for any woman depressed by struggling with weight problems.

Gamblers Anonymous and Gam-Anon, 17/23 Blantyre Street, Cheyne Walk, London SW10 (01–352 3060).

Portia Trust, 15 Senhouse Street, Maryport, Cumbria CA15 6AB for Midlands and Northern England (090 081 2114), and,
Bassanio Trust (Southern England), 35 Woodberry Way, London N12 0HE (01–445 0581), for those who get into trouble with the law through stress and depression.

SHAC, 189a Old Brompton Road, London SW5 0AR (01–373 7276) for advice on housing problems.

Hysterectomy Support Group, Rivendell, Warren Way, Lower Heswall, Wirral, L60 9TU (051–342 3167).

Incest Survivors Campaign, c/o A Woman's Place, Hungerford House, Victoria Embankment, London WC2.

Mastectomy Association, 26 Harrison Street, Kings Cross, London WC1H 8JG (01–837 0908).

Relatives of the Mentally Ill, 7 Selwyn Road, Cambridge CB3 9EA.

Mothers Apart From Their Children (MATCH), BM Problems WC1N 3XX (01–892 9949).

National Council for One-Parent Families, 255 Kentish Town Road, London NW5 2LX (01–267 1361).

Organisation for Parents Under Stress, 26 Manor Drive, Pickering, N. Yorkshire YO18 8DD. 24-hour Helpline (PACT) 01–668 4805.

Parents Anonymous helpline (01–263 8918), 9 Manor Gardens, off Holloway Road, London N7 6LA.

Patients Association, Room 33, 18 Charing Cross Road, London WC2H 0HR (01–240 0671).

British Pregnancy Advisory Service, Austy Manor, Wootton Wawen, Solihull, West Midlands B95 6BX (05642 3225) for problems connected with pregnancy including abortion, sterilisation, artificial insemination.

PMT: The Unrecognised Illness by Judy Lever with Dr M. Brush and Brian Haynes, New English Library.

Prime Time by Helen Franks, Pan, for women experiencing a mid-life depression.

Rape Crisis Centre, P.O. Box 69, London WC1X 9NJ (01–837 1600).

Step-families Association, Maris House, Maris Lane, Trumpington, Cambridge CB2 2LB (0223 841306).

Institute of Psycho-Sexual Medicine, 11 Chandos Street, Cavendish Square, London W1M 9DE.

Association of Sexual and Marital Therapists, P.O. Box 62, Sheffield S10.

Redwood, 83 Fordwych Road, London NW2 3TL (01–452 9261) for national network of women's sexuality and assertiveness groups.

Woman's Experience of Sex by Sheila Kitzinger, Dorling Kindersley.

Treat Yourself to Sex by Paul Brown and Carolyn Faulder, Penguin, self-help for common sexual difficulties.

Sexual and Personal Relationships of the Disabled (SPOD) 286 Camden Road, London N7 0BJ (01–607 8851).

Albany Trust (01–730 5871) helps with psycho-sexual problems, especially those of sexual minorities.

Action on Smoking and Health, 27–35 Mortimer Street, London W1N 7RJ (01–637 9843).

Women's Aid Federation (England), 374 Gray's Inn Road, London WC1 (01–837 9316 and 01–837 3762 for London enquiries only) for women suffering from violence.

National Association of Widows, c/o Stafford District Voluntary Service Centre, Chell Road, Stafford ST16 2QA (0785 45465/56532).

AUSTRALIA

Australian National Association for Mental Health, Suite 3, 194 Miller Street, North Sydney NSW 2060 (02–929 7993).

Psychiatric Rehabilitation Association, 153 George Street, Redfern NSW 2016 or P.O. Box 182, Redfern NSW 2016 (02–699 6868).

Women's Health Care Association Inc., Women's Health Care House, 92 Thomas Street, West Perth WA 6005 (09–321 2383).

Family Foundation (SA) Inc., 597 South Road, Everard Park, SA 5035 (08–293 5181).

Family Life Movement of Australia, 150 Concord Road North, Strathfield, NSW 1237 or P.O. Box 143 Concord NSW 2137 (02–73 2136).

Family and Personal Counselling Service, 24 Anthill Street, South Hobart, Tasmania 7000 (002–23 6041).

The Good Neighbour Council, 67 Castlereagh Street, Sydney NSW.

National Marriage Guidance Council – eight main branches across Australia.

Marriage Guidance Council of New South Wales, 226 Liverpool Road, Enfield NSW 2136.

Marriage Guidance Council of Victoria, 46 Princess Street, Kew, Victoria 3125.

Queensland Marriage Guidance Council, 159 St Pauls Terrace, Brisbane QLD 4000.

Tasmanian Marriage Guidance Council, 24 Anthill Street, Hobart, Tasmania 7000.

Canberra Marriage Counselling Service, 8 Petrie Plaza, Savings House, Canberra City A.C.T. 2601.

Marriage Guidance Council of Western Australia, 32 Richardson Street, West Perth. W.A. 6005.

Marriage Guidance Council of South Australia, 55 Hutt Street, Adelaide S.A. 5000.

Marriage Guidance Council of Northern Territory, 62 Cavenagh Street, Darwin N.T. 5794.

Childbirth Centre, 3 Union Street, Paramatta, NSW 2150.

Childbirth Education Association, P.O. Box 58, Forest Hill 2087.

Royal Society for Welfare of Mothers & Babies, 32 Grosvenor Street, Sydney NSW 2000 (02–27 2210).

Parents without Partners Aust. Inc., c/o National Secretary, P.O. Box 22, Weston NSW 2326 and International: 138 Flinders Street, Melbourne, Vict. 3000 (03–63 1746).

Birthright, G.P.O. Box 4134, Sydney 2001, supports one-parent families.

The Samaritans
  P.O. Box 991, Albany, W.A. 6330 (098–414 777).
  P.O. Box 480, Kalgoorlie, W.A. 6430 (090–214 111).
  60 Bagot Road, Subiaco, Perth, W.A. 6008 (09–381 5555 &
  5725) and Samaritan Youth Line same address (09–381
  2500).
  P.O. Box 2113, South Hedland, Port Hedland, W.A. 6722
  (091–721 999).

Lifelink, P.O. Box 228, Launceston, Tasmania 7250 (31 3355
& 39 1770).

Association of Civilian Widows, 3 Forth Street, Kempsey
2440, NSW.

National Association for Loss and Grief and the Outstretched
Hand Association, c/o Sister Williams, Director of Nursing,
Mount Carmel Hospital Pty. Ltd., Crews Street, Seven Hills
2147 or Miss D. Culpan 283 Cavendish Road, Coorparil
4151, Queensland. Help and support for the dying, their
families, the bereaved.

Preventive Services, 24 Done Street, (or P.O. Box 300)
Arncliffe 2205 NSW.

Victorian Association of Citizens Advice Bureau 356
Collins Street, Melbourne, Victoria 3000 (03–602 3299).

Alcoholics Anonymous, 363 George Street, Sydney, NSW
2000.

Association of Relatives and Friends of the Emotionally and
Mentally Ill, 15 Cromwell Road, South Yarra, Victoria 3141.

Association of Relatives and Friends of the Mentally Ill, 311
Hay Street, Subiaco, Western Australia 6008.

Biofeedback Meditation Relaxation Centre, 165 Adderton
Road, Carlingford, NSW 2118.

The Compassionate Friends (bereaved parents support
group), 8 Kyeema Parade, Belrose, NSW 2085.

Help Call Service, 1A Hamilton Street, Mont Albert, Victoria
3127.

Life Line, 16 Hamilton Place, Bowen Hills, Queensland 4006.

Life Line Centre, 210 Pitt Street, Sydney NSW 2000.

Lone Parent Self-Action Group of Australia, 21 Thurana Street, Stafford, Queensland 4053.

Marriage and Family Counselling Service, 262 Pitt Street, Sydney, NSW 2000.

Melbourne Family Therapy Centre, 349 Union Road, Balwyn, Victoria 3103.

Parents Centres Australia, 45 Hunter Street, Sydney, NSW 2000.

NEW ZEALAND

Mental Health Foundation of New Zealand, The Secretary, P.O. Box 37–438, Parnell, Auckland 1, New Zealand. Will give information to anyone on their nearest Parents Centre/ Parentline / Marriage Guidance / Citizens Advice / Family Planning/Lifeline/Womens Health Centre and will help set up discussion groups, self-help support groups, etc.

Advisory Committee on Women's Affairs, State Services Commission, Private Bag, Wellington, NZ.

Society for Research on Women in New Zealand, Box 13–078, Johnsonville, Wellington, NZ.

Motherhood of Man Movement, Inc. Box 68–083, Auckland, NZ.

National Old Peoples Council of New Zealand, P.O. Box 27–271, Wellington, NZ.

Parents Centre Organisation, P.O. Box 11, Wellington, NZ.

Council for the Single Mother and her Child, Box 47–090, Auckland, NZ.

Solo Parents NZ Inc., 11 Bonnie Glen Crescent, Upper Hutt

Birthright, P.O. Box 347, Wellington, to support one parent families.

The Samaritans
9 Herbert Street, Greymouth, South Island & P.O. Box 448 (6611)
69 Woburn Road, Lower Hutt & P.O. Box 27294 (664 591 and 664 252)
YMCA Premises, Church Street, North Masterton (81259)
15 Amesbury Street, North Palmerston & P.O. Box 1963 (74400)

Hakiaha Street, North Taumaranui (6664)
P.O. Box Brooklyn 6309, North Tauranga (81001)
120 Guyton Street & P.O. Box 4116 Mid-Av. P.O. North Wanganui (55090)
Cathedral Building, Molesworth Street, & P.O. Box 12041, North Wellington (49600)

Lifelink, c/o Social Service Centre, Rotorua, NZ.

60's-up Movement, P.O. Box 3143, Auckland, NZ.

Cruse, for the widowed:
Mrs M. Wallace, 8 White Street, Taradale, H.Bay.
Mrs R. E. Flannery, 18 Menin Road, Onekawa, Napier.
Mrs M. Drown, 303 Sylvan Road, Hastings.

New Zealand Widows' & Widowers' Association Inc., Mrs Valerie Austin, P.O. Box 12–160, Wellington. For help and advice – branches throughout New Zealand.

Womens Refuge Inc., Box 8044, Dunedin, NZ.

SOUTH AFRICA

South Africa National Council for Mental Health, P.O. Box 2587 Johannesburg, 2000 South Africa.

South African Psychological Association, P.O. Box 4292, Johannesburg, 2000 South Africa.

National Council for Marriage and Family Life, 114 MBA Building, 413 Hatfield Street, Pretoria, South Africa.

Institute for Child and Adult Guidance, Rand Afrikaans University, P.O. Box 524, Johannesburg 2000 South Africa.

National Council of Women of S.A., 532 CTC Building, Plein Street, Cape Town 8001 South Africa.

Council for Social and Associated Workers, Private Bag X348, Pretoria, South Africa.

The Samaritans P.O. Box 2201, Bloemfontein, Orange Free State (83000) 305 Old Mutual Building, Oxford Street, E.L. 5201 (27559).

Lifeline Head Office, Roelandts Street, Cape Town, South Africa.

Pathways Institute of Thanatology, Jenny Kender, P.O. Box 391037, Bramley, Johannesburg 2018 South Africa. For information on problems related to dying, death and bereavement, widow-to-widow basis.

Widows Information Service (Weduwees-Inligtingsdieds), Mrs Hilda Powell, 501/503 CTC Building, Plein Street, Cape Town, 8001 South Africa.

Notes

1. *The Health and Fitness Handbook,* ed. Miriam Polunin, Sphere, London.

2. Drs Thomas Holmes and Richard Rahe of Washington Medical School.

3. Adapted from *A Woman In Your Own Right,* Anne Dickson, Quartet.

4. *The Social Origins of Depression,* George Brown and Tirril Harris, Tavistock Publications, 1978.

5. *Trouble with Tranquillisers,* Release Publications.

6. *Good Health Guide,* Open University in association with the Health Education Council and the Scottish Health Education Unit.

7. Adapted from the Redwood manual for women's sexuality courses by Anne Dickson.

Index

Index